Haunted
Ohio

Haunted Ohio

Ghosts and Strange Phenomena
of the Buckeye State

Charles A. Stansfield Jr.

Illustrations by Heather Adel Wiggins

STACKPOLE
BOOKS

For my nearest and dearest—
Diane, Wayne, Paul, Beth,
Jordan, Aidan, and Bryce

Published by
STACKPOLE BOOKS
5067 Ritter Road
Mechanicsburg, PA 17055
www.stackpolebooks.com

Printed in the United States of America

10 9 8 7 6 5 4 3 2

FIRST EDITION

Design by Beth Oberholtzer
Cover design by Caroline Stover

Library of Congress Cataloging-in-Publication Data

Stansfield, Charles A.
    Haunted Ohio : ghosts and strange phenomena of the Buckeye State / Charles A. Stansfield Jr. ; illustrations by Heather Adel Wiggins. — 1st ed.
        p.   cm. — (Haunted)
    Includes bibliographical references.
    ISBN-13: 978-0-8117-3472-1 (pbk.)
    ISBN-10: 0-8117-3472-2 (pbk.)
    1. Haunted places—Ohio. 2. Ghosts—Ohio. I. Wiggins, Heather Adel. II. Title.
BF1472.U6S727   2008
133.109771—dc22
                                                                    2007037709

Contents

Contents

Introduction

HAUNTED OHIO IS A UNIQUE TOUR OF THE BUCKEYE STATE, ONE THAT
crosses both space and time. This collection of tales of the supernatural illustrates the geography and history of the great state of
Ohio. The stories of ghosts, witches, monsters, and aliens from
outer space take you to every part of Ohio, from the shores of Lake
Erie to the banks of the mighty Ohio River, from the Appalachian
Hills to the western flatlands, from the great cities to remote farms.
Every part of the state has its tales of the supernatural, traditions of
haunted buildings, ghostly apparitions, UFO appearances, and scary
witches. You will meet the ghosts of the rich and famous—presidents, first ladies, and military heroes—as well as the shades of
ordinary folks such as schoolteachers, firefighters, and coal miners.

Just why do we find tales of ghosts, witches, and monsters so
fascinating? Why are there so many popular movies, television
shows, books, and articles with supernatural themes? This fascination with the realm of spirits is a constant and major theme
throughout history. Great writers from William Shakespeare to
Stephen King have intrigued and entertained us with stories in
which ghosts and witches play important roles.

What scares you? Did you really catch a glimpse of a strange figure on the stairs, or was it only your imagination? Are those creak-
ing sounds up in the attic just an old house responding to the wind
or something much more disturbing, some supernatural presence?

It is said that a wise man once was asked if he believed in
ghosts. "No," was his reply, "but I am afraid of them." Are you one

of the many who would agree, not certain that there are spirits out there haunting the living, but not sure that there aren't?

Whether you happen to be a true believer in the supernatural, a firm skeptic, or part of the uncertain, unconvinced middle, you can enjoy a good story. In this guided tour of haunted Ohio, you will meet both legendary figures like Mike Fink and Johnny Appleseed and historic personages like abolitionist John Brown and sharp-shooter Annie Oakley. You will encounter Satan himself, in several guises, as well as heroic clergymen, courageous warriors, and a gentle poet. Supernatural snakes, a toad that was really a witch, a truly scary phantom cat, and a dog that chased ghosts likewise all await your acquaintance. Enjoy your visit with Ohio's many ghosts, monsters, devils, and witches. And lock all your doors at night.

Lakeshore

THE LAKESHORE REGION OF OHIO STRETCHES ALONG THE SHORES OF Lake Erie from the Pennsylvania border to the Toledo metropolitan area at the Michigan border. This region includes the great industrial center of Cleveland as well as many charming lakeshore resorts, including the islands north of Sandusky and Port Clinton. This land of Indian warriors, great industrialists, smugglers, and sailors has its dark side, with stories of the supernatural including a presidential ghost, a vampire cat, and a mysterious fortune-teller.

A Presidential Ghost

Is it possible for one ghost to haunt several different locations? And if it is, do the spirits travel instantaneously? Many believe that ghosts choose to appear, if at all, at places that had special meaning to the living person or where the body is buried.

The phantom of James A. Garfield, twentieth president of the United States, reportedly has been seen, at various times, in the White House; in his last home before becoming president, in Mentor, Ohio; and in Hiram, Ohio, where he was a student working his way through college as a janitor, and later as an English teacher and college president. His ghost, some claim, has also been seen at Elberon, on the New Jersey shore, where he died.

A number of recent sightings suggest that at least on occasion, Garfield's ghost chooses to haunt his tomb in Cleveland's Lakeview Cemetery. Some think that his spirit began to haunt the tomb after Garfield's beloved wife, Lucretia, joined her martyred husband in death, having outlived him by thirty-six years.

All deaths by violence are tragic, but James Garfield's agonizing death was especially sad in that better medical care—or more exactly, less intrusive medical care—could have saved his life. It is a curiosity that out of four U.S. presidents who have been assassinated, two were from Ohio—James Garfield and William McKinley. McKinley and Garfield also shared other common circumstances: Both were wounded by the assassin's bullet, and both survived for a time, though critically wounded—McKinley for a few days, and Garfield for eighty days. Whereas Lincoln and Kennedy both suffered massive head wounds that they could not have survived, McKinley probably could have been saved if modern antibiotics were available, and Garfield definitely would have lived if his infection had been controlled by antibiotics.

Although many Civil War veterans at the time were walking around with bullets lodged in them, Garfield's doctors probed endlessly with nonsterile fingers and instruments trying to retrieve the bullet. In doing so, they spread the infection, which eventually overwhelmed the president. At his trial, the assassin, Charles Guiteau, commented that it was Garfield's doctors, not the bullet, that really killed him. True, but it was beside the point. Guiteau was executed.

Now, almost 130 years after his agonizingly prolonged struggle with infection, James Garfield's ghost is said to roam about his impressive memorial, a tower 50 feet in diameter and 180 feet high, with a chapel in which his casket—and perhaps his ghost—can be viewed.

The Vampire Cat

A farmer near the charming little town of Geneva learned about vampires the hard way—he inadvertently created one. All he wanted to do was to raise an aggressive house cat to control mice in his barn.

Most farmers find it wise to keep a few cats around the farm. Fred Ross was no exception. After his best mouser died of old age,

Fred was lucky enough to find a stray kitten abandoned by the side of the road. It was pathetic. Its eyes barely open, it was weak from hunger. Did this half-dead furball have a future as an aggressive hunter of vermin?

Fred had an inspiration. Instead of coddling it with warm milk and canned cat food, the kitten would be raised on blood and guts. A butchered hog provided plenty of fresh gore. Much to Fred's delight, the helpless kitten quickly grew into a mean killing machine. The cat, now named Tiger, began proudly delivering dead mice, rats, rabbits, and birds to the Rosses' front doorstep, the feline equivalent of bragging.

It took Fred a while to realize that Tiger was not eating much of his prey, but in fact always drained the little corpses of every drop of blood. Tiger certainly was death on mice and rats, but soon he was attacking larger and larger animals for their blood. Small dogs, piglets, lambs, even raccoons became his victims. Fred, by now openly fearful of Tiger, began going to local slaughterhouses to obtain buckets of blood to satisfy the cat, now grown to monstrous size.

Finally Fred observed Tiger stalking children walking to school. Obviously Tiger had to go to cat heaven—or, rather, cat hell. Fred's shotgun ended Tiger's career as a vampire. But only temporarily. To his horror, Fred saw Tiger, fur matted with blood and earth, rise from his shallow grave and begin stalking a large dog. Hastily reading up on vampire lore, Fred melted some old silver coins into a bullet mold. The silver bullets worked, and Tiger's corpse was burned. The whole neighborhood relaxed, and everyone agreed that milk, not fresh blood, was the proper food for kittens.

Blood Will Tell

The small city of Portsmouth is perhaps most famous for its massive, two-thousand-foot-long flood wall, decorated with fifty-two murals depicting three hundred years of history of the area. One story that does not appear in the murals is the sad saga of the bloody attic wall. Only one man saw the persistent, telling blood stain, and that was the murderer. This tale has been called Ohio's version of Edgar Allan Poe's classic horror story "The Tell-tale Heart."

What happened to young Marjory Weatherby is just as horrible as any of Poe's masterpieces. Marjory's mother had died recently of typhoid, a disease frequently epidemic in the mid-nineteenth century. Her father, to put it bluntly, decided that ten-year-old Marjory would be a suitable substitute for her mother in the marriage bed. For months, poor Marjory was shamefully and repeatedly abused.

Finally, Marjory's mind snapped under the stress. She attacked her sleeping father with a kitchen knife, but lost the struggle. Her bloodied father overwhelmed her and killed her. With callous calculation, he placed her body in the bathtub, slit her throat, and hung her by her feet. Handy with tools, he decided to conceal the corpse in the house. He built a false wall in front of a wall in the attic, creating a space to hold poor Marjory. Then he spread word that Marjory had decided to move in with her older sister in Cincinnati.

When he checked his remodeling job in the attic to see if the paint had dried, he was horrified to see blood seeping from the new plaster. Hastily he destroyed the stained plaster and remade the wall. A new paint job followed in a week. But frustratingly, blood once again stained the wall concealing Marjory. He repeated the tear-down and replacement operation twice, to no avail. Finally he decided to panel the wall in thick oak planks, which seemed to work.

Unnerved, the child molester and murderer put his house up for sale. A prospective buyer, who happened to be the chief of police, wanted to inspect the whole house. When the tour reached the attic, the murderer saw that yet again, blood was leaking from the new paneling. "No!" he screamed. "I drained all her blood. This cannot be!" He began tearing out the false wall, revealing the mummified body of his daughter.

After hearing a full confession, the police chief locked the culprit into a cell. "The funny thing is," he said, "there wasn't any blood in sight. Not a drop." Apparently the only stains were on the father's conscience.

Tall Corn and Tall Tales

Folks around Parkertown still tell stories about the local superhero version of Paul Bunyan or Mike Fink: a farmer by the name of James McCord. McCord was the greatest farmer in Ohio—he'd tell you so himself. Often. Now Ohio farmers grow tall corn, but James McCord grew the tallest of them all, and he certainly told the tallest stories.

Some believe that McCord's spirit visits the area still, dropping into local taverns to trade tall stories for tall cold ones from generous listeners. So if a sunburned farmer in worn coveralls starts telling wonderful stories at the bar, buy him a drink. You just might be seeing the ghost of a legend.

Jim liked to tell how he grew ears of corn so huge that he couldn't load them into a wagon. So, one by one, he yoked a team of oxen to each ear and dragged the ears like logs into the barn. Once, when a storekeeper ordered fifty pounds of corn, Jim refused, saying he wasn't going to split an ear for such a small order. Such tall corn naturally produced tall corn-fed poultry. McCord had a rooster, Old Buckeye, that was so tall he had to eat his corn off the barn roof.

McCord was a great marksman. Once, while out hoeing his cornfield, he heard a grinding noise overhead. Grabbing his rifle, he quickly shot down a flock of grindstones and sold each at a nice profit.

It goes without saying that Jim was a man of great strength. Once a neighbor passing by was astonished to see McCord pick up a full-grown horse and throw it the length of the pasture, then repeat this feat. Asked what he was doing, Jim replied that he was practicing pitching horseshoes. When his neighbor suggested first removing the shoes from the horse, McCord retorted that that wouldn't be any fun—anyone could pitch the shoes *off* the horse.

Like other farmers, McCord was plagued by rats getting into his corn bin. A neighbor observed McCord unloading a caged mountain lion down at the freight depot. "Starting a circus, Jim?" he inquired. "Heck, no. My corn kernels are so big only rats the size of possums come round my barn," Jim replied. "Still, that's a mighty big cat you've got there, Jim. How will you keep him under control?" "Well," said McCord, "you should see the dog I'm getting to keep the cat respectful like!"

Now, aren't stories like that worth a free drink? Even if it is for a ghost!

The Free-Loving Ghosts

The tiny community of Berlin Heights is, unaccountably, about seventy miles northwest of Berlin, Ohio. And obviously it's a great deal farther from the original Berlin. Berlin Heights has its own special claim to fame in the spirit world: It hosts not just one ghost or two, but a whole troop of them. This happy group likes to stroll about town at dusk on summer evenings, waving greetings to townsfolk and passersby. And they're naked and not at all self-conscious about it.

If you are going to encounter a ghost, or two, or more, you could do worse than to come across these cheerfully unclothed spirits of the free lovers who many years ago made Berlin Heights their home. Once they fully realized the group's eccentricities, the town's more tradition-minded citizens became wary of the free lovers. These merry advocates of free love enthusiastically sought new converts among what was then a staunchly conservative farm community. Fruit growing recently had been introduced along Ohio's lakeshores, where the water's accumulated summer warmth helped prolong the growing season into late October. Vineyards thrived and apple orchards flourished. The newly arrived free love group, to the surprise and dismay of their new neighbors, proved to be hardworking farmers and astute businessmen. They paid their bills promptly, always paid their taxes, contributed to local charities, and tried to be good neighbors to the disapproving old settlers.

The problem was, thought the more conservative villagers, that the free love crowd wasn't shy about anything. They freely acknowledged their unorthodox view of marriage—a kind of love communism, they called it. The only rules governing sex seemed to be that both participants be willing and that everyone help, with both time and money, in providing for offspring whose male parentage might be uncertain. The free lovers were not shy about discarding clothing around their houses when weather permitted. Even more infuriatingly, they were not at all shy about expressing their political and social views at every opportunity. They loved an audience and delighted in debate.

Finally, shortly after the Civil War, growing general disapproval of the free love contingent forced most of the group to sell their property and move on. But as a final gesture of defiance of the uptight community standards, they paraded nude through the village, much enjoying the outrage of their staid neighbors.

Every summer since, the spirits of the free love movement repeat their naked march. Should you see them, just step aside. They've never threatened anyone, and some are just supernaturally cute.

The Corpse Who Killed a School

The little community of Willoughby, about eighteen miles east of downtown Cleveland, used to have a medical school. In fact, it was one of the first medical schools in Ohio, founded in 1834. It grew rapidly, so that by 1843, it boasted an enrollment of two hundred students—a fairly large school at the time. But then the growing school was killed, never to arise again. It was destroyed by a dead man.

In the early nineteenth century, the medical profession was undergoing a major change in the way future doctors were educated. Previously, just about anyone could decide to be a doctor and set up an office. Some were graduates of prestigious medical schools, such as those already established in Boston, Philadelphia, New York, or Baltimore. But others had merely taken a quick correspondence course on combining a good bedside manner with liberal prescriptions of alcohol-based tonics. There was a need to establish higher standards of medical training, with a strong foundation in human anatomy and physiology. Scientific study required cadavers, skeletons, and preserved organs. To help the living, medical students needed to learn from the dead.

Unfortunately, the medical school demand for fresh corpses far exceeded the legal supply of unclaimed bodies from poorhouses and hospitals and executed criminals. Desperate to obtain bodies for teaching and research, medical schools learned not to ask too many questions when purchasing corpses delivered late at night to their backdoors. Grave robbers were known as "resurrection men," as at their hands the dead appeared to rise out of their coffins. Members of many a grieving family planted flowers and erected tombstones over graves that, unknown to them, were empty.

At least one desecrated body—or, rather, its ghost—fought back. The story is that a certain Mrs. Tarbell, newly widowed, was visited a few days after her husband's funeral by a horrifying apparition. It was her dead husband, naked and carrying his severed head in one hand and his heart in the other. Over his shoulder were ropelike intestines. "Won't you help me, darling?" pleaded the gruesome phantom. "I'm being butchered at the medical school and cannot go to my eternal rest." Mrs. Tarbell ran out screaming into the night, arousing her neighbors to form an angry mob. The outraged friends, relatives, and neighbors, convinced that their town's medical school had either arranged the grave robbery or knowingly accepted a stolen corpse, invaded the college building. The howling throng ransacked every room, searching for what was left of Mr. Tarbell. They smashed furniture and equipment and tossed medical specimens, skeletons, and odd fragments of cadavers out the windows into the street. Willoughby Medical College never recovered from this blow to its physical plant and its reputation, closing forever a few years later.

Some say that for decades afterward, the naked, partially dismembered corpse of Mr. Tarbell strode the streets of the town, bewailing his disheveled state of unrest. This dead man had succeeded in killing a college.

Incidentally, several professors from the defunct Willoughby Medical College went on to establish Case Western Reserve University Medical School of Columbus, and other former faculty members founded the Starling Medical School, which now is part of the Ohio State University. It is a good bet that those gentlemen never bought cadavers from "resurrection men" again.

The Financier's Ghost

A cluster of small islands, including North Bass, Middle Bass, South Bass, and Kelley's Island, lie in Lake Erie north of Sandusky. One of the smallest among them is called Gibraltar, and it is said to be haunted.

Arrogant self-assurance seems to radiate from this ghost as he appears to stride across the little island, which now serves as a state fisheries and conservation experiment station. Gibraltar Island, like its famous namesake, rises sharply above the waves. It seems to guard the western portion of Put-In-Bay Harbor. Eight-acre Gibraltar once was the private property and summer home of one of Ohio's more controversial sons, Jay Cooke. It is Cooke's phantom that is said to haunt his favorite home, only a few miles from his birthplace in Sandusky.

Jay Cooke's career as an investment banker made him one of the famous—or is it infamous—"robber barons" of the period of extravagant multimillionaires that Mark Twain called the Gilded Age. In life, Cooke was not exactly popular. Many blamed him, fairly or unfairly, for single-handedly bringing about the Panic of 1873 when his banking firm collapsed in bankruptcy. Jay Cooke had invested unwisely in overpriced railroad securities, and the panic his company's failure seemed to precipitate ruined many businesses and took jobs away from scores of thousands. Cooke went broke himself, briefly, before bouncing back, richer than ever. Many other victims of the financial panic were not so fortunate and blamed Cooke for their plight.

On the other hand, Abraham Lincoln paid tribute to Jay Cooke as the man who helped finance the Civil War. In 1861, at the age of forty, Cooke undertook the responsibility of selling an extraordinary half a billion dollars' worth of government bonds, a truly staggering amount at the time. Cooke became America's top salesman by organizing twenty-five hundred bond agents across the nation. Every bond was sold.

Jay Cooke was a complicated man, to say the least. Arrogant self-made millionaire, ruthless stock market manipulator, reckless gambler with other people's money, and patriotic bond salesman extraordinaire—Cooke was all of these.

There is a story that when Jay was only fourteen, his father joked with his sons that they were all on their own, as their house had been sold and they were all homeless. Apparently convinced that his father was serious, Jay went out and got a job that same day, and he never stopped working until he died—the typical hard-driving "type A" personality.

You might encounter the ghost of Jay Cooke striding purposefully across his island, business papers clutched in one hand, a glass of champagne in the other. Don't get in his way. Cooke's ghost, as in life, is a man on a mission who does not tolerate distractions.

A Spirited Argument

Located in Lake Erie north of Sandusky is a group of islands—Kelley's, the three Bass Islands, and a scattering of smaller rocky islets. Notable for two happy activities, vacations and winemaking, these sunny realms of fun also have a dark side. The delightful tourist village at Put-In-Bay on South Bass Island features one of the nation's most imposing battle monuments, celebrating Oliver Hazard Perry's famed victory in a naval battle to control Lake Erie during the War of 1812. The grounds around this monument are said to be haunted by the ghosts of American and British sailors who died in the battle. These ghosts are restless and unhappy, often heard arguing heatedly over war strategy and international politics. They are said to be so angry and frustrated for two reasons: Enemies in life, they have been buried side by side, and their bones do not lie in their original graves but were unwisely disturbed, moved into the shadow of the huge Perry Victory Memorial.

Oliver Perry was only twenty-eight years old when he was placed in command of a U.S. naval squadron built for him at Erie, Pennsylvania. His mission was to engage and defeat a flotilla of British warships on the lake. Perry's success was made possible by his never-give-up attitude. When his flagship *Lawrence* was disabled and its guns silenced in a ferocious encounter with the British, Perry and his officers rowed to another American ship, *Niagara,* and then boldly took on four enemy ships at the same time and forced their surrender. Perry's message to General William Henry Harrison, who later became the first of seven Ohioans to be elected president, was short and to the point: "Dear General—We have met the enemy and they are ours. Two ships, two brigs, one schooner and one sloop. Yours with great respect and esteem, O. H. Perry."

The day after Perry's victory, September 12, 1813, the six British and American officers killed in battle were buried side by side at Put-In-Bay, with full military honors. The ghostly appearances of the arguing enemies are said to have begun when, a century later, the bodies were dug up and moved to the base of the 352-foot-high Perry monument. It is thought that many ghosts are the result of graves being disturbed and bodies being moved. The moving of their bones plus the fact that these six ghosts may well have killed one another seems to have led to some very restless spirits.

Blacksnake Sails On

Many a yachtsman or fisherman has been startled to see an incredibly fast boat flash by him or her late on moonless nights. The mystery boat carries no running lights, which is illegal. But then, the Coast Guard rule that all craft, no matter how small, must display lights at night, especially while under way, is the least of the laws being broken here, for the silent, swift, darkened boat that sails

Lake Erie around the popular vacation resorts of Kelley's Island and the three Bass Islands is the ghost of a notorious rumrunner, known in those parts as *Blacksnake*.

"*Blacksnake*" was not its legal name, for the boat was registered as *Ruby*, honoring the Captain's wife. But to the locals, she was *Blacksnake*, as she was painted a dull black so as to be almost invisible on dark nights, which was when her owner, Captain Scott, used her for rumrunning during Prohibition. Captain Scott liked the nickname, because real black snakes are notoriously nasty snakes that can give a mean bite, though they are nonpoisonous. Black snakes are said to sometimes drop out of trees onto people just to entertain themselves.

National Prohibition in the 1920s created lucrative opportunities for smugglers to import booze from Canada, Mexico, the Bahamas, Cuba, and Bermuda. North Bass and Kelley's islands are only about seven miles from Pelee Island, Canada, so liquor smugglers, known as rumrunners, could purchase alcohol legally in Canada and give it a short boat ride to Ohio's Lake Erie islands, and then on to the mainland. Fortunately for the smugglers, these islands are honeycombed with caves, which made ideal hiding places for alcohol on its way to thirsty customers ashore.

The Coast Guard tried hard to catch the rumrunners, so the smugglers' boats had to be fast and hard to see at night. Rumrunners developed a peculiar, specialized type of craft called cigarettes, which were long and slender in profile. They usually were powered by one or two military surplus aircraft engines, which propelled them through the water much faster than Coast Guard cutters could manage. They had shallow drafts to enable them to come close in to the shore for unloading at deserted beaches, and their decks were close to the waterline to give them a low profile, making them difficult to spot on the lake. Though perfect for smuggling, their design made these craft very vulnerable to being swamped by high waves, as in storms.

Late in the season of 1926, the Coast Guard was out in force on the waters just north of Kelley's Island. Captain Scott decided to risk a run on a dark and stormy night, hoping to avoid capture, as the more wary Coast Guard captains would sensibly stay in port. It was a fatal decision. *Blacksnake* left Canada's Pelee Island with a full load of scotch whiskey, bound for a secluded beach on Kelley's

Island. The boat never reached her destination. To this day, many boaters in the waters around North Bass and Kelley's islands swear they saw *Blacksnake* come flying by them in the middle of the night, eternally bringing her cargo home to Ohioans appreciative of the world's best whiskey. If you should spot *Blacksnake* late some night, follow the local custom of raising a glass in her honor—filled with the best scotch, of course.

Thus Spoke the Unborn

Many years ago, a Cleveland gypsy fortune-teller enjoyed a reputation as a provider of unusually detailed and accurate predictions of the future. Establishing herself in a dingy storefront in a decidedly low-rent district, she billed herself as a European psychic and offered a full range of traditional gypsy fortune-telling techniques— crystal ball, palm reading, and tea-leaf reading. Her gimmick (though none would use that word to her face) was that she cheerfully admitted to her clients that she herself possessed no special powers of foretelling the future. Her insight came from her unborn child, she claimed, as she pointedly patted her swollen midsection.

The gypsy would explain that the unborn, existing in a state of complete innocence, insulated from the suspicion, greed, and deceptions of the world, have the purity of mind necessary to see the future clearly. "I'm only voicing what my unborn child sees," she would say. Her reputation and list of clients grew in proportion to the accuracy of her predictions. More than one speculator in the stock market swore that he multiplied his fortunes by following the gypsy woman's insights into future economic conditions. Once a plainly skeptical young woman was advised by the gypsy that she would soon meet a handsome stranger, an old familiar standby of psychic lore. Sure enough, the very next day saw an encounter with a good-looking English aristocrat, visiting Cleveland for the first time. A successful marriage followed shortly, producing a flood of eager new clients for the fortune-teller.

On another occasion, a newlywed young man, a sailor on a Great Lakes ore carrier, consulted the gypsy about his future children. "Of children you'll have none," she warned, "if you sail again with your ship." Shaken, he decided to switch to a land job, working on the docks rather than as a sailor. On its next voyage, his former ship disappeared in a freak summer storm, along with its entire crew.

The amazing accuracy of her future predictions, however, could not distract her clients from noticing the obvious: The lady seemed to be permanently pregnant. How could a pregnancy, albeit with a very special and spiritually gifted fetus, last so long? Months stretched into years, and still the gypsy attributed her descriptions of the future to her gifted unborn. Her patrons, faced with unavoidable evidence of fraud, drifted away, sometimes reluctantly, as the predictions attributed to the imaginary fetus remained remarkably reliable.

The gypsy never changed her story, and her figure retained the familiar bulge of impending motherhood. When at last she died, the medical examiner found that, as a skeptic and a man of science had expected, the old woman was wearing a pouchlike harness under her clothes, which explained her permanent "pregnancy." But there was one last surprise from the gypsy: Inside the cloth pouch were the bones of a slightly premature infant. Hers was a child born not into life, but into death. Did her dead child somehow have insights into a future it would never know? Was the gypsy telling the truth, that her unborn child possessed special powers?

We will never know. The old gypsy and her infant's bones were buried together.

Margaret's Cross

"Blood will tell" is a phrase familiar to fans of tales of the supernatural. This is a story in which blood does play a role, if silently, in "telling" about the character—and the future—of those who come in contact with a certain steel examining table in a charitable free clinic in Cleveland a generation ago.

Financially supported by several churches and other social agencies, the clinic served people in a very poor and, too often, violent neighborhood. The old steel table that received the sick and wounded had many baptisms of blood in those circumstances. One of the most faithful workers at the clinic was a young medical student who was considering a vocation as a nun. She was a beautiful woman, the inner beauty of her soul matching her pretty face, but her outward beauty led to her tragic end.

Leaving the clinic late one evening, the earnest young volunteer, Margaret, was attacked in the parking lot before she could reach the safety of her car. Her assailant, intending to rape her, held a knife to her throat as he fumbled with her clothing. Margaret fought back valiantly, defending her honor as vigorously as possible.

The would-be rapist slashed her repeatedly with the knife, inflicting many deep cuts on her arms as she sought to fend him off. Finally the brute realized that Margaret's screams would attract attention, and he abandoned his now-helpless prey and retreated. Margaret was carried into her own clinic and laid on the examining table. She lay with her wounded arms outstretched, blood pouring from her neck, face, arms, and torso. A lot of blood, too much blood. She died on that old steel table, an innocent victim of wanton brutality, defending her virtue to the last.

But that is not the end of the story. When Margaret's body was removed to the morgue, a routine cleansing of the venerable examination table failed to remove the bloodstains. The steel table, which had been designed to repel all manner of stains, and indeed had effortlessly shed gallons of blood, stubbornly retained traces of Margaret's blood—and in the pattern of a large cross, reflecting the position of her bloody head, torso, and outstretched arms. Only the most generous and determined repeated applications of bleaching disinfectants could fade "Margaret's cross," as the stain became known, though a barely visible outline persisted.

Then an even stranger part of the story began. Whenever patients bled on the table, their blood would replenish Margaret's cross, reinforcing and deepening the cruciform stain. The clinic's doctors and nurses soon observed that when the fresh blood was cleaned off the steel tabletop, an easy cleanup, of whatever quantity of blood, signaled that a patient would soon recover and was in no mortal danger. But if the bloody cross persisted through the attempt to remove it, the patient was best transferred to a hospital, as his or her life was in danger. On rare occasions, Margaret's cross not only reappeared in fresh blood, but seemed to shimmer with an inner light and was a particularly stubborn stain to eliminate. These occasions seemed to signal that the blood had been shed by a truly evil person—a person later identified as a murderer, rapist, arsonist, or other criminal.

What caused the repeated renewal of the bloody cross? Could there be a scientific explanation? As is well known, iron is an important component of human blood, which is why anemic or iron-deficient people take iron pills. Had the innocent blood of Margaret, whose character was almost saintlike, somehow magnetized the cruciform stain her blood created, attracting the iron in fresh blood to revitalize her cross? Unfortunately, the steel table was destroyed when fire swept though the clinic, so Margaret's cross cannot be further tested.

The Phantom Ambulance

A family from New Jersey had an interesting, and probably life-saving, experience while driving along the shores of Lake Erie on U.S. 6 west of Cleveland. These New Jerseyans, who wish to remain anonymous, encountered fog along the lakeshore, which is not unusual. It can move in quickly and reduce visibility to a few feet.

These tourists were cruising along admiring the scenery and not noticing the occasional wisps of mist in low-lying areas. Their minds were focused on a planned visit to Cedar Point Amusement Park, with its world-famous roller coaster. Suddenly flashing red and amber lights appeared in their rearview mirror. They pulled over onto the road shoulder to allow a speeding ambulance to flash past.

As they slowly edged back onto the highway, a billowing fog bank suddenly engulfed them. Visibility fell to nearly zero. As they crept into the dense mist at low speed, barely visible and stationary taillights ahead warned them to stop, and just in time. A multivehicle crash, caused by the fog, had littered the highway with broken cars and people. They carefully pulled over to the edge of the road and set out some emergency flares that the father, a member of a volunteer fire department back home, always carried.

Within minutes, a state police cruiser arrived on the chaotic scene. The trooper summoned more help, then complimented the tourists on setting out flares, probably preventing an even larger pileup. But how did the New Jerseyans avoid becoming part of the multiple crash scene? "We had pulled over to the edge and stopped to allow the ambulance to pass," they explained, "so we were moving slowly back into the traffic lane when the fog moved in." "What ambulance?" asked the officer. "There is no ambulance here, and one could not have moved past the crash scene without hitting wreckage." The lucky family decided that a guardian angel must have sent a phantom ambulance to warn them of the dangers ahead.

The Devil and the Gambler

Tales of the supernatural often offer a moral. Such is the case of a half-forgotten legend about the dangers of an addiction to gambling. It seems that twin boys were born to a middle-class family in Cleveland around 1880. The boys, whom we'll call Adam and Matthew, were fraternal twins, quite different in appearance and, as it turned out, in temperament, personality, and fate.

As frequently happens with twins, the first to be born, Adam, turned out to be the more dominant personality. Always more aggressive, Adam was more adventurous, while Matthew was a quiet intellectual. Adam became a wealthy man by speculating in coal properties in southeastern Ohio, buying interests in Great Lakes iron ore carriers and taking a chance on that rapidly growing new industry, oil. Matthew, in the meantime, became a minister and eventually a bishop in the Methodist church.

Adam's fortune had been built on his willingness to take chances on new enterprises. Sadly, his attraction to risk degenerated into an addiction to gambling. He would bet on anything—horse racing, sports contests, and cards. Card playing became a compulsion, and his suburban mansion became notorious for the high-stakes gambling marathons Adam loved.

The nature of the games changed as they went from friendly social pastimes to tensely competitive contests. His friends dropped away as Adam became an abusive card shark, in the language of the day.

His brother, Matthew, the Methodist bishop, regularly implored Adam to change his ways and stop his increasingly reckless gambling. Adam's compulsion simply grew worse. Finally, on the morning of Good Friday, Matthew visited his brother to invite him to attend church services together. "No," said Adam. "I've a mind to play cards today." "On Good Friday?!" exclaimed his shocked brother. "Surely you wouldn't gamble on this day of all days!" "Of course I will," replied Adam. "One day is like another to me. I'm only happy at the card table."

But Adam didn't find it easy locating someone to sit down with a deck of cards. His usual partners declined, citing the religious significance of Good Friday. Even Adam's servants, usually eager to please the boss, refused. Frustrated, Adam finally screamed out, "Will no one cut the cards with me?" At that moment, a tall, handsome stranger, dressed elegantly all in black, appeared at the door. "Lucifer is my name, and poker is my game," he announced, "but I only gamble for high stakes." Mentally tallying his vast wealth, Adam asked, "How high?" "Your immortal soul," was the reply. Behind closed doors, the game began. An hour later, Adam's servants heard an agonized and unholy scream. Bursting into the room, they found Adam dead, his face contorted in fear. His opponent had vanished, as had Adam's soul. Folks should be careful when and with whom they gamble.

Granny Knows Best

This tale was the unhappy experience of one Slovenian-American family living in Cleveland. Frankly, they'd like to forget the whole thing. If only Granny had come by sooner.

The weird, frightening phenomena began soon after Uncle George died in the house, the victim of a sudden and overwhelming heart attack. Within a few hours of the unexpected death, windows in the house began to rattle without any apparent cause. One by one, every mirror in the house shattered for no reason, at least none that the householders could understand. As family or visitors entered or exited the house, they felt a jostling at the door, as though an unseen person were trying to squeeze past them and go outside. What on earth was happening?

More unusual occurrences followed within a few days of the uncle's death. A friendly card game at the kitchen table ended when the cards kept flying off the table. When tuned to a light comedy, the new television in the living room went blank.

Invited to the house for lunch following the graveside service, the family's oldest living member, Granny, supplied some answers. Was the family following the ancient Slovenian traditions after a death in the house? Her question was met only by blank stares. "What traditions?" asked the younger generations. First of all, advised Granny, the spirit of the deceased wants to leave the house within twenty-four hours of death, but it cannot open doors or windows by itself. If weather permits, at least one window or door must be left open so that the spirit can depart on a forty-day journey on earth before moving on to the spirit world. During this last sojourn, the spirit must attempt to right any wrongs it committed in life. At the moment of death, all mirrors in the house should be turned to the wall. If the ghost of the deceased sees the absence of its reflection, it will smash the mirrors in frustration. Also, it is disrespectful to enjoy games or entertainment while the spirit is still in the house, hence the problems with playing cards and watching TV. Lastly, a bucket of water must be left outside the door so that the Grim Reaper can rinse his bloody scythe and go on his way without reentering the house, which could cause another death there.

The family took Granny's advice and followed the old customs. Apparently the uncle's ghost also followed tradition and left them in peace afterward.

***OHIO* IS THE IROQUOIS WORD FOR "FINE (OR BEAUTIFUL) RIVER," AND** indeed it is a fine river. It provided a natural route for pioneers who floated down the mighty river on their way to opportunities in the West. The Ohio Valley region stretches from the Pennsylvania border to the eastern edge of the Cincinnati metropolitan area. Ohio's oldest cities, such as Marietta and Gallipolis, are in this long, sinuous region, and the valley is also home to some of the state's oldest ghost stories. Prehistoric Indians built great mounds in the valley, some of them serving as burial sites, similar to Egyptian pyramids and thought to be just as haunted.

Watch Out for Mike Fink

Watch out for Mike Fink. He was fearsome in life and is doubly so as a ghost. Many a boatman on the Ohio River has sighted the ghostly legendary keel boatman on the river, and old Mike also has been known to appear on the riverbanks and in old river towns like Marietta and Gallipolis.

Superheroes are not just a twenty-first-century phenomenon. Americans always have delighted in tales of larger-than-life, incredibly bold and strong folk heroes. The Great North Woods of the upper Midwest gave us Paul Bunyan; the Ohio Valley produced Mike Fink.

Mike described himself, it is said, as being "half wild mustang and half cockeyed alligator." He was a hardworking, hard-living, hard-drinking boatman along the Ohio when the valley was a wild frontier, from the end of the American Revolution through the 1820s. Americans were moving west, and nature provided a magnificent highway to get there—the mighty Ohio River. Crude, flat-bottomed barges known as flatboats carried people as well as livestock, flour, salt pork, and lumber, on down the river from Pittsburgh to Louisville to St. Louis, even all the way to New Orleans. The boatmen who steered the flatboats downstream, around sandbars, across rapids, and past hostile Indians, were a tough lot. They knew it and were not bashful about making sure that everyone knew it. They loved to boast, and their humor was based on wild exaggeration.

Mike Fink was an expert shot. He was the best marksman who ever lived—or ever lived on as a ghost. Mike also was a thirsty man, who much appreciated a drink or two, or three or four. A favorite trick of the man, and now his ghost, involved getting a free drink. Mike would appear suddenly in the doorway of a frontier cabin or at the gangplank of a moored flatboat. "Would you by chance be able to spare a glass of whiskey?" he'd inquire politely. If his new host provided a glass promptly, then Mike would be all smiles, sharing a joke or two before taking his leave. Should his host unwisely refuse, Mike would draw his gun and shoot the cork off the man's jug or bottle, after which Mike would drain off every last drop of whiskey. Once, when a barrel of whiskey stood behind an unwilling host, Mike drilled a hole in the barrel with a bullet, then drank from the resulting stream of the "good stuff." "Had enough?" inquired his outraged and unwilling bartender. "Sure," replied Mike. "If I'd wanted more, I'd have shot the hole lower!"

And so, if a bearded, somewhat unkempt stranger with a frontiersman's rifle slung over his shoulder approaches you one evening and requests a glass of whiskey, pour him one. Make it a full glass. Smile. Better to be a gracious host to Mike Fink's ghost than to refuse him a drink. Or two.

The Legend of the Shape-Shifting Witch

Nearly two centuries ago, a witch lived on the outskirts of Marietta, Ohio's oldest community. Or perhaps we should say alleged witch, for there never was any solid evidence that old Betty Brown was anything but an eccentric old woman.

Witch or not, Betty was a lonely person, as she did not encourage visitors to her ramshackle old house. Other than maintain a kitchen garden, Betty did not farm her land, yet she always had the money necessary for her purchases in town. Curious about her source of income, her neighbors began to spread the rumor that old Betty had a crock of gold hidden away, a gift from her supposed master, Satan himself.

Betty lived at the end of the golden age of witchcraft, or at least the golden age of popular belief in, and unreasoning fear of, witches. Only a generation or two earlier, accused witches were tortured and killed for their alleged allegiance to the Prince of Darkness. Most people actually believed that witches not only existed, but could shape-shift. Interestingly, native traditions from American Indians to Central Europe to Africa included shape-shifting— the ability of witches, vampires, or devils to change form from a person to a wolf, bat, owl, or cat.

If, indeed, Betty Brown were a witch, then perhaps she too could shape-shift. The rumor about Betty's hidden crock of gold attracted the attention of the more adventurous and criminal-minded members of the community. Two would-be thieves decided to sneak into Betty's house one evening to look for her gold. At her front gate, however, they were confronted by the biggest, meanest, most aggressive alley cat they'd ever seen. Snarling, hissing, and spitting, the creature attacked the trespassers, who then suffered painful bites and scratches. The two finally drove off the cat with a hail of stones, one of which hit the cat's left eye and persuaded the animal to retreat at last.

Soon everyone in town had heard about the incident. When Betty showed up at the general store, shopping basket in hand, ready to do her weekly shopping, the townspeople were stunned by her appearance: Betty had a large, ugly bruise around her left eye. Was the feisty "watch cat" that so aggressively protected Betty's house actually Betty herself? Had the old witch shape-shifted? Needless to say, no one ever again tried to burglarize the witch.

The Warrior's Magical Worm

Many a folktale carries a cautionary message: "Be careful what you wish for." Such is the theme of a half-forgotten story of the Indian warrior's magical worm. This supposedly happened in the late eighteenth century in the vicinity of Gallipolis, the second-oldest permanent European settlement in Ohio.

The Indian brave had earned his name, Thundercloud, by having a temper like a summer thunderstorm—unpredictable, violent, and of short duration. Patience was not among his virtues, yet he liked to go fishing, a sport that would seem to require patience in large quantities.

The traditional Indian fishing technique featured the use of weirs, rows of sticks driven into the river bottom in shallow water in a V formation. The fishermen would wade out into the river and churn the water, driving fish into the point of the V-shaped trap, and then spear them.

Thundercloud wanted to try European-style fishing, with a baited hook at the end of a line. He dug a supply of worms and set out to catch dinner. Black bass, muskies, perch, pike, and both bullhead and channel catfish make the Ohio River a fisherman's paradise. But not for Thundercloud on that day. Crafty fish repeatedly stole his bait right off the hook. He was having a frustrating day. Impulsively, Thundercloud called out to the evil spirit, the Prince of Darkness, "Give me a worm that will catch a fish!" At that moment, a footlong worm appeared at the end of his line. It lunged at a nice bass, wrapped around the hapless fish, and threw the creature into Thundercloud's canoe. Soon six big fish lay in the canoe, and Thundercloud decided to call it a day. The big worm curled up on the riverbank and pointedly stared at his catch. Taking the hint, the grateful Indian tossed the largest fish to the magical worm, which caught it in razorlike teeth and gulped it down.

When Thundercloud showed up at the river's edge for another day of angling, the worm already was curled up in his canoe, eager to go fishing. Oddly, the worm seemed to have grown another twelve inches in length. That day, the ferocious worm tossed some huge channel catfish into the canoe. At day's end, Thundercloud had to reward his fishing partner with two of the largest catch.

Soon the ever-growing worm, by now looking more like a giant snake, was demanding more than half of the day's catch. Within a week, Thundercloud was starting the day's fishing by sacrificing small game—rabbits, ducks, opossums, raccoons—to his fanged fishing companion. When the magical worm, by now eight feet long, began demanding a daily offering of a whole deer, Thundercloud finally realized this satanic and insatiable creature must be destroyed.

Standing on the banks of the Ohio, Thundercloud began hacking at the demonic worm with his war tomahawk. To his horror, though, soon after his tomahawk sliced through the worm, the separated segments magically rejoined. Was Satan's worm indestructible? Then Thundercloud had an inspiration. He moved the scene of the struggle out into the great river. Now, as his sharp tomahawk sliced away at the worm, the separate pieces were carried away by the river's strong current before they could reunite.

At last an exhausted Thundercloud had defeated the magical worm. It is said that he never again went fishing, nor did he ever again ask for help from the evil spirit.

Boat of Blood

A narrow canal boat moves along the Ohio and Erie Canal through the Scioto Valley just north of Portsmouth. Drawn by mules walking along the towpath, the boat travels at a leisurely two to three miles per hour. Its slow progress is accompanied by the most bloodcurdling scream, as this is a boat of death, of murder most foul. And it is a ghost, for the canal is long abandoned, the canal boats having since rotted away, leaving only the legend of the murder boat.

The misty apparition of the canal boat is glimpsed only rarely these days, usually around dawn or dusk. The grisly affair of Sally Hunter began with a kidnapping and ended with the discovery that a serial killer may have been operating on the canal for years.

The Ohio and Erie Canal linked Cleveland, Columbus, and Portsmouth. Completed in 1832, the canal supported an economic boom across central Ohio. The canal boats transported hogs, grain, lumber, and sundry goods, along with passengers who were in no particular hurry. Hundreds of boats crowded the canal in its heyday, and hidden in plain sight among the crowd was the *Betty Lou,* an innocuous-sounding name for a boat that was to become infamous in the annals of crime.

Betty Lou was owned and captained by Bart Anderson, a hulking brute of a man whom no one trusted. Their instincts were right, for Bart may have been one of the most notorious serial killers of all time. Operating a canal boat that was more or less constantly moving gave Bart a nearly perfect situation for his crimes. In May 1834, he grabbed a twelve-year-old girl, Sally Hunter, from the banks of the canal at a quiet anchorage just south of Columbus. Poor Sally evidently was, by Bart's own confession, raped and murdered aboard the boat. He dismembered her body and fed it to the hogs that were the cargo, then threw the bones overboard in the dark of night.

But a passing mule driver spotted some human bones in the hog pen that had escaped Bart's notice. A police search of the *Betty Lou* turned up a drawer full of grim souvenirs of many murder victims, including jewelry and bloodstained clothing. Bart readily admitted, indeed boasted about, killing more than a dozen victims in the past year as his boat glided across the state. The ghost of the *Betty Lou* is still seen cruising the derelict canal, bearing its cargo of horror accompanied by unearthly screams through the quiet countryside.

The Strangled Cat

Fair warning: The story of how this ghost came to be is scarier even than the ghost itself, which is pretty gruesome. This phantom, the sight of which can freeze one's blood in the veins, has been known to appear in a residential neighborhood close to downtown Marietta.

The large tomcat growls menacingly from its perch atop a stone garden wall. Its razor-sharp teeth are bared, its ears flattened against its head, and its eyes widen in a yellow-green stare challenging the passersby. So far, this sounds like any ill-tempered cat defending its turf. This ferocious feline is distinguished, however, by mud caking its black fur and a noose of ragged rope about its neck. Anyone brave enough to approach this fearsome creature will then hear an unearthly yowl from the cat as its back arches in warning. If encountered late at night, the usual time of its appearance, a faint phosphorescent glow can be seen on the tips of its ears, tail, and whiskers.

The best advice is to run, not walk, away, for you have met the phantom strangled cat of Marietta. The story is that a generation ago, a very disturbed boy, whom we'll call Dan, lived in the neighborhood. Dan was a nasty little boy, mean toward any living creature. As a toddler, he attacked rather than petted dogs and cats. As he grew older, smaller children as well as animals learned to stay well away from Dan. His cruelty became legendary. One of his last acts against animals, before he was jailed for life on a murder charge, involved hanging a cat—the cat whose ghost still prowls Dan's onetime neighborhood.

Animals, particularly cats, often seem to have a sixth sense of potential evil. This neighbor's big tomcat was especially alert to Dan's psychotic potential for violence and calculated cruelty. The cat sometimes would stalk Dan, suddenly jumping out at him from a hiding place and growling before taking off. Dan and the cat displayed a mutual hatred that ended in terror.

One night, Dan managed to grab the cat, and despite being badly bitten and scratched in the effort, he got a noose around the frantically struggling animal. Dan hanged the cat from a large tree, then buried it in a shallow grave in his backyard. But the cat didn't stay in its grave. Its dirt-caked form, still wearing its rope noose, stalks the neighborhood yet, looking for Dan. Don't get in its way.

The Traitor's Ghost

A most unhappy, tormented ghost haunts the Ohio Valley in the area between the old town of Marietta and Blennerhassett Island, about ten miles downstream. This terminally depressed ghost, with a long, sad face covered in tears of bitter regret, is that of Harman Blennerhassett. Harman was once a very wealthy man, a member of an Irish aristocratic family that owned a great deal of land in Ireland. He and his wife, Mary, both were well-educated, brilliant intellectuals who came to Marietta to begin lives full of promise. Why, then, is Blennerhassett's ghost that of a miserable, frustrated, and broken man, an utter failure at everything he attempted? The answer lies in his involvement in a vast conspiracy against the

United States, a traitorous plot led by the infamous Aaron Burr. Burr was the highest-ranking government official ever to be tried for treason. Blennerhassett was Burr's close associate—or, some say, puppet—in this failed scheme.

Blennerhassett and his wife arrived in Marietta in 1798. Soon he purchased a 170-acre tract on the island that now bears his name. He built a famous mansion on the island, furnishing it with the best of everything imported from the East Coast and Europe. The Blennerhassetts entertained lavishly, establishing themselves as the social leaders of frontier society.

One day in 1805, an important guest arrived on an elaborate houseboat—Aaron Burr, vice president of the United States. Burr was a brilliant man who had graduated from Princeton University at age sixteen. He had been a Revolutionary War hero, governor of New York, and senator, and had just lost a close election to Thomas Jefferson. In those days, coming in second in a presidential race made you vice president—a job that Burr hated.

Aaron Burr dreamed of establishing an empire of his own in the West, with its capital to be New Orleans. He persuaded Harman Blennerhassett to finance fifteen barges filled with arms and ammunition to be sent down the Ohio and Mississippi rivers to New Orleans and used in a war against the United States. When news of this conspiracy reached Jefferson, the president ordered the arrests of Burr and Blennerhassett. The conspirators fled downriver but were captured at Natchez.

Supreme Court Chief Justice John Marshall presided over a trial at Richmond in which Burr and Blennerhassett were freed because of insufficient evidence. But during the trial, Blennerhassett's mansion was looted by patriots certain of his guilt, even though unproven. A flood destroyed what was left of the once-grand estate, and Blennerhassett and his wife fled, first to Mississippi, then to Canada, and finally back to Europe. Harman never regained his reputation or his fortune. Two of his children died in infancy, two were hopelessly insane, and the fifth was a notorious alcoholic. Until Blennerhassett met Aaron Burr, everything he did was a glorious success. But after he joined Burr's ill-conceived traitorous plot, everything he attempted ended in disaster. Is it any wonder that Harman Blennerhassett's is a most unhappy ghost?

The Rebs Are Coming!

Ohioans were very much divided politically during the Civil War. Before the war, Ohio citizens were very active in the Underground Railroad, transporting runaway slaves to Canada. When President Lincoln asked the nation for 75,000 volunteers, Ohio responded with 30,000—twice the state's quota. But as the war wore on and many of Ohio's sons returned home severely maimed or in coffins, the "Peace Democrats," better known as Copperheads, who sympathized with the South, grew in influence under the leadership of Dayton's Clement Vallandigham. In 1862, Ohio sent a mostly Democratic group to Congress. Eventually Vallandigham was arrested for treason and exiled to the Confederacy. Ohio ended up supplying 340,000 troops to the Union armies—more than half its male citizens of military age.

It was a Confederate general, John Morgan, who really unified Ohioans against the Confederacy. He did so by striking fear in the hearts of Buckeye state residents when he invaded and terrorized southern Ohio. Morgan led 2,460 Confederate cavalry into southern Indiana, then eastward toward Cincinnati in July 1863. When 50,000 state militia assembled to defend Ohio's Queen City, Morgan led his force around the city and on up the Ohio River Valley, looking for an opportunity to escape back across the mighty river.

Morgan's Raiders traveled fast, stealing fresh horses whenever they could, along with food, guns, and anything else they saw when they descended suddenly on small towns and isolated farms. They seemed to be always a few hours ahead of their pursuers. Until July 9, 1863, that is, when Morgan's force was almost surrounded by Union troops, and Union gunboats cut off any possible retreat across the river. This struggle, at Buffington Island, was the only major Civil War engagement in Ohio, producing 700 Confederate prisoners but ending in General Morgan's escape. He later was captured and imprisoned at Columbus State Penitentiary, from which he escaped by tunneling under the walls.

Many a valley resident swears that the ghosts of Morgan's Raiders still ride at night, their rifles held at the ready as their horses race along country roads, looking for a defenseless farm to raid. The gray Confederate uniforms seem to merge with the river fog as word spreads: "The Rebs are coming!" Yes, the Rebs are coming, but now they are mere phantoms, not the fearsome invaders they once were.

Johnny Appleseed Is Still At It

There is no doubt that Johnny Appleseed was a real person. Some Ohioans believe that his ghost is just as real.

This is a harmless, well-intentioned spirit. As with many ghosts, this one simply is following the lifelong role of the once-living person. The phantom Johnny Appleseed most often appears in Ohio's beautiful countryside in spring, the best time to plant his gifts of apple seeds. Some believe that Johnny's ghost more recently has expanded his wandering to the suburbs of cities, where an apple tree or two in a backyard or lawn can add to the quality of life, with its gifts of lovely white flowers in spring and its juicy fruit.

Johnny Appleseed's ghost, like the living man, cares nothing about appearances. As often as not, he is barefoot. His clothing consists of cast-offs, gifts from people in exchange for apple seeds or tiny seedlings. In cooler weather, Johnny wears a burlap sack with cutout holes for his head and arms. The supernatural Johnny continues his old habit of wearing a tin cookpot as a hat, cushioned by a brim made of cardboard. Large leather sacks filled with apple seeds hang over his shoulders.

The phantom Johnny is short, of average weight, with long, straggly hair and a sparse, untrimmed beard. He'll offer a handful of seeds as a gift but will gladly accept a few slices of bread in return. He'll politely refuse any meat, as Johnny believed that killing any animal was wrong, and that the bountiful earth produced vegetables, grains, fruits, nuts, and roots in abundance for all God's children.

Johnny Appleseed's real name was Jonathan Chapman, believed to have been born in Boston in 1775. His first recorded visit to Ohio was in the spring of 1806, when he sailed his canoe down the Ohio River to Marietta, then up the Muskingum River, visiting every farmstead with his gift of seeds. Eventually he covered the entire state in his travels, and then extended his treks into Indiana, where he died in 1847. Apparently his spirit still continues the good work the man started.

Incidentally, if Johnny's ghost offers a warning of impending danger to you and your family, along with a handful of seeds, it would be wise to listen. The living Johnny Appleseed was strongly opposed to violence of any kind. During the War of 1812, the British persuaded some Indians to become allies against American settlers on the frontier. Marauding bands of warriors would attack remote farms, killing and burning. The Indians never harassed Johnny Appleseed, who lived by gathering wild plants, didn't carry a weapon, and seemed intent only on distributing apple seeds. But Johnny kept track of hostile groups and made it his business to warn endangered settlers of any threat to their lives. Ill-intentioned travelers still catch the attention of Johnny Appleseed's spirit, and his ghost may deliver a warning of approaching danger along with his free seeds.

The Love Boat Sails On

They called them "love boats," but in reality they were lust boats. These boats plied the Ohio River back in the rowdy frontier days of the late eighteenth and early nineteenth centuries. America was on the move westward, and the Ohio conveniently flowed in that direction. Nature's great highway charged no money tolls, but the price of passage in terms of blood, sweat, and tears was high. Life was rough, tough, and often short. The rugged men who guided the flatboats—great barges hastily built of timber that handled clumsily in the great river's surging currents—prided themselves on working hard, cussing hard, living hard, and playing hard. Their "playing" frequently took place in lowdown dive bars, and aboard the love boats, with their cargoes of prostitutes, cheap whiskey, and loathsome diseases.

Today many people who work on, play on, or live near the river swear they've seen phantom love boats, drifting with the current or tied up in some secluded cove. They carry the customary running lights of red for port (left) and green for starboard (right), but their distinguishing features are the additional red lights above every door and in every window. They are floating "red-light districts," and their heyday was the early 1800s, when the river was populated by adventuresome, hard-brawling men, far from home, lonely and desperate for companionship of the female variety.

The ghostly love boats, looking like crude shacks on rafts, aglow with their red lights, appear swiftly and silently out of the river mist. As they float close by, the faint sound of raucous laughter, drunken partying, and fiddle or banjo music might drift across the water. Those who captain the tugs pushing trains of barges on the river have learned not to bother taking panicky evasive action when a ghostly love boat appears on a collision course. They know that at the last possible moment, the crimson lights will wink out as the phantom craft evaporates like fog on a sunny morning.

The oceans have their legends of *Mary Celeste* and the *Flying Dutchman;* the Ohio has the equally mysterious and evasive love boats. Should you encounter the red glow of a ghostly love boat, just maintain a steady course. A brief prayer might be in order too.

The Light in the Attic Window

Uncle Tom's Cabin was a literary triumph and a runaway best-seller in America before the Civil War. But it was much more than dramatic fiction—it was a political force in itself, often credited with rousing public opinion against the evil institution of slavery and helping precipitate the Civil War.

You'll find *Uncle Tom's Cabin* on the fiction shelves, but at least part of the book is based on a real incident. In the book's most dramatic scene, the heroine, Eliza, manages to escape her pursuers by leaping from one ice floe to another across the river separating free territory from slave territory. The real Eliza, on whose exploits Harriet Beecher Stowe based that scene, was a runaway slave heading for sanctuary in Ripley, Ohio, at John Rankin's home, which still stands as a museum.

Legend has it that the Reverend John Rankin was a leading abolitionist, very active in the Underground Railroad, which transported runaway slaves to freedom in Canada. Rankin's house is perched at the edge of the bluff high above the river town of Ripley, across the Ohio River from the slave state of Kentucky. Anyone convicted of aiding runaway slaves was subject to severe punishment, so abolitionists learned to be cautious and secretive. Only when it was reasonably safe to approach his house would the Reverend Rankin place a bright light in his attic window. This light pointed directly at the North Star, the beacon of freedom followed by the desperate runaways.

A set of stairs, some stone, some wooden, climbed the steep slope from the valley. These were, according to tradition, used by the runaways and are still known as Jacob's Ladder. It is on Jacob's Ladder that some claim you can see the ghosts of escaping slaves struggling up the hill toward the sanctuary of John Rankin's house. These spirits are most likely to appear on moonless nights and when the light in the attic window shines in reassurance. Should you happen to spot the phantom runaways breathlessly climbing Jacob's Ladder, just silently wish them well. You have witnessed history—or at least, the ghosts of history.

The Dog That Chased Ghosts

A family in Portsmouth tells the story of how their dog, Cosmo, took on the job of chasing ghosts. The family, whom we'll call the Taylors, moved into an old house on the edge of town. Only a low stone wall separated their property from a large cemetery. The Taylors' new neighbors, whose land also bordered on the cemetery, told them nervous jokes about spirits visiting their house on occasion, specifically their kitchen. They said that mysterious sounds of dishes, glasses, and tableware being moved about often came from their kitchen late at night. In the morning, dirty dishes and glasses testified that unseen and uninvited guests had raided their refrigerator. Were the residents of the cemetery actually dropping in for a drink and a snack?

Then the Taylors began to fear that they, too, had been targeted as unwilling hosts by hungry and thirsty spirits. The occasional late-night sounds and morning appearances of used dishes and glasses in a kitchen that had been left spotless the previous evening unnerved them. Why would the dead need or want even small quantities of food and drink? But then, why do the living expect ghosts to behave rationally or bother with any rules? The Taylors began to think about moving to a house farther removed from the dead.

Then Cosmo entered their lives, a gift from friends whose family pet had produced a litter of six puppies. Cosmo, named after a character on a TV comedy series, was a purebred Bouvier des Flandres, a breed of Belgian sheepdogs. Bouviers, however, were not primarily concerned with herding sheep. Their role as working dogs was to provide protection against predators. Known for their courage, Bouviers would face down a wolf or bear with unflinching bravery. As often as not, even bears would back off from a confrontation with a Bouvier, apparently realizing that victory would come at the price of some serious damage to themselves. Not particularly cuddly, Bouviers are very loyal and protective, especially of young children, whom the dogs probably regard as similar to lambs.

Cosmo's first few nights in the household were uneventful, as the freeloading ghosts visited only randomly. When, at last, strange sounds emanated from the kitchen, Cosmo sprang into action. Barking furiously, the dog charged into the darkened room. After a few moments of frantic barking, all was quiet. Never again were the Taylors bothered by ghosts. Cosmo just wouldn't stand for it.

Pale Death

Gallipolis, "City of the Gauls," was founded by French immigrants in 1790, making it Ohio's third-oldest permanent European settlement. A half-forgotten legend makes Gallipolis the home of Ohio's most chilling vampire tale. No, vampires are not just found in Eastern Europe, as in the classic story of Dracula. Many different peoples from many lands have traditions of vampires, including the French. This is the story of Denise LaFarge, whom many believe truly was a vampire.

Louis and Denise LaFarge were among the first settlers of Gallipolis. They no sooner had cleared their land and built a cabin on it than Denise began to look sickly. Every day, she seemed to grow more pale, more listless. Her skin, once a healthy pink, took on a translucent pallor, her blue veins looking like a map of a river system. She took to her bed, no longer able to walk. Finally Denise died, but of what cause? A rumor began to circulate that she had been the victim of a vampire. At first her husband, Louis, was the prime suspect. But he passed the ultimate test for vampires: He did not shrink away from the Holy Crucifix. Indeed, he took to wearing one around his neck. In time, Louis remarried, a young farm girl in the bloom of youth, Marie. Marie was robustly healthy—the opposite of poor Denise in her final weeks.

But then Marie began to look unhealthy. Her weight dropped and her energy flagged, much like poor Denise. Despite the devoted care of Louis, Marie soon was buried beside Denise. The local opinion was that Marie, like Denise, had died of loss of blood, victim of a vampire. But who was the vampire? Then the townsfolk remembered that the victims of vampires became, after death, vampires themselves.

They decided to dig up Denise's coffin. The corpse turned out to be perfectly preserved. Indeed, it looked healthier than ever, with rosy skin and full red lips. To everyone's horror, the corpse was found to have a mouth full of fresh blood. In the French tradition, there was only one course of action in dealing with an immortal vampire. Denise's dead body was tied to a stake and burned. As the flames leaped up, Denise's eyes flew open, and an unearthly scream was heard. The ashes were dumped into the river so that the waters would disperse them, preventing any possible reassembly. Just to be sure, Marie's body also was burned. But who infected Denise? No one knows. Perhaps the vampire still roams at night, searching for its next victim.

The Phantom Barge Mate

Many passengers aboard the luxury passenger barge *River Explorer* enjoy spending some time in the pilot lounge at the vessel's bow. There guests, known as "barge mates" to the friendly crew, can have an unobstructed view of the river and its busy traffic. Radio transmissions between *River Explorer*'s captain and other barges, boats, and lock tenders at the many dams are broadcast into the lounge, which is equipped with books of detailed navigation charts. Some passengers probably secretly fantasize that they are piloting the vessel as it cruises the Ohio River from its juncture with the Mississippi to as far upstream as Pittsburgh or Charleston, West Virginia. Whether or not they are wannabe river pilots, à la Mark Twain, most passengers daily spend a pleasant hour or so enjoying their front-row seats observing the changing panorama of the great river.

One passenger in particular seems to really delight in perching on the well-padded stools of the pilot lounge, using binoculars to observe wildlife and water traffic. He smiles and nods politely to new arrivals at the large windows but does not speak. It could be said indeed that this gentleman haunts the lounge, as he really is not there—he is a ghost.

As many fellow passengers have discovered, the phantom barge mate will disappear if another guest attempts to engage him in conversation. It seems that the phantom barge mate simply wishes to be alone. The elderly man always is neatly dressed in casual attire, with a yachtsman's cap on his gray head. Interestingly, he never shows up in the dining room. Apparently, being a ghost, he has no need for food, even gourmet food. The ghost barge mate has been known to appear nightly in a far corner of the theater balcony. It seems he enjoys each evening the live performances of local musicians playing bluegrass, country, or jazz music.

Just who is the phantom passenger, and why is he aboard *River Explorer?* Though the official stance is "What phantom passenger?" many longtime staff report having glimpsed him briefly. Some barge personnel assert that the ghostly apparition may be that of a widower, a retired schoolteacher who, in life, was so charmed by the leisurely pace and luxurious accommodations aboard *River Explorer* that he took at least six cruises on it. In death, with his spirit free to roam anywhere he pleases, why not take some more cruises and relive the best memories of his old age? Indeed, why not? Bon voyage!

Cincinnati

and the Southwest

CINCINNATI, THE QUEEN CITY OF THE OHIO VALLEY, DOMINATES THE southwestern Ohio chain of cities in the Miami River Valley, including Dayton and Springfield. Once the largest city west of the Appalachians, Cincinnati's industries attracted many Germans, Italians, and African Americans, all bringing their own traditions of ghosts and witches. Dayton, an early center of aircraft design and development, has a long tradition of UFO sightings—evidence perhaps of extraterrestrials' intense interest in humankind's first ventures into the air.

The Storytelling Spirit

Dayton's Woodland Cemetery is notable for two reasons: It is a beautiful place of landscaped hills, flowering dogwoods, even a lake, and it is the final resting place of Dayton's most famous citizens, such as Wilbur Wright. There is also a third reason, at least according to some students of the supernatural: One of its most famous inhabitants is a ghost. This phantom, it is said, likes to perch atop his own tombstone, especially at dusk on fine spring and summer evenings, telling stories and reciting poetry to an audience of other spirits who gather around. According to his tomb-

stone, this gentle ghost is that of the famed African American poet Paul Laurence Dunbar.

Born in Dayton in 1872, Paul Dunbar early displayed his literary talents. The only African American in his high school class, Paul was president of the Literary Society and editor of the school paper. At age twenty-one, he published his first volume of verse, followed eventually by four more books of poetry. He also wrote four novels, a musical play, and many short stories. While working on his first book, he supported himself by operating an elevator in a downtown Dayton office building.

Dunbar's fame took him to New York and all the capitals of Europe, where his talent was honored, but he came home to Dayton for the final six years of his sadly short life. Dunbar died in 1906 at age 34, but his irrepressible spirit lives on, materializing to weave a poetic spell over his ghostly audience.

Even if you are not so fortunate as to witness his ghostly performances, you can learn more about Paul Laurence Dunbar and see his original manuscripts at his last home, now a museum, on North Summit Street in Dayton. A plaque on the wall of his house reads, "Because I had loved so deeply, because I had loved so long, God in His great compassion gave me the gift of song."

The Cider-Drinking Ghost

Can drinking hard cider cure a cold? Evidently not, as testified by the story—and the ghost—of William Henry Harrison, ninth president of the United States.

Harrison's ghost, it is said, occasionally haunts his tomb, which stands atop a hill overlooking the Ohio River at North Bend, west of Cincinnati. This phantom appears near sunset, seated, gazing out at the lovely view. The spirit, wracked by evidently painful spasms of coughing, pauses often to sip from a large jug of hard cider. Hard cider and pneumonia played important roles in the saga of William Henry Harrison, who was, before the election of Ronald Reagan, the oldest man ever to occupy the White House. He still holds the record for the shortest presidency—exactly thirty days, before dying of pneumonia contracted during a lengthy inaugural address in a freezing rain.

Harrison joined the Army at age eighteen and distinguished himself as an Indian fighter and in the War of 1812. He served in the Ohio legislature, in Congress as a representative and a senator, and also was ambassador to Colombia. When he ran for president against the incumbent Martin Van Buren, his opponents derided Harrison as the "log cabin and hard cider" candidate. Harrison turned this slur into an advantage. It was said that when both men campaigned in Ohio, Van Buren drank tea from English china cups, while Harrison drank hard cider from an earthenware jug. Which would a man trust in the White House—an effete easterner who sipped tea or a rough-hewn warrior statesman who drank right from a jug of honest hard cider? The answer was clear to a majority of voters.

And so his ghost sits today, jug in hand, watching the river traffic and remembering a long career of service to his country capped by only a month as chief executive. Perhaps you'd like to toast William Henry Harrison—with hard cider, of course.

The Preacher and the Hounds of Hell

Many years ago, a Springfield preacher had an unforgettably terrifying experience with the Hounds of Hell. His encounter with Satan's minions came about when the pastor responded to the pleas of the newest members of his congregation—a professor, newly appointed to the faculty at Wittenberg University, and his wife.

The professor was convinced that he and his wife had moved into what turned out to be a house cursed by the Devil. Would the preacher be kind enough to confront the evil that seemed to permeate the house? "Of course, I'll try to help," said the man of God. "But what makes you think an evil spirit is present?"

"Dishes and glasses fly off the table and smash. A pot of boiling water suddenly fell off the stove, nearly scalding my wife. Fresh milk turns sour in an instant when brought into the house. Candles light themselves, then snuff themselves out. Silver and brass tarnish in seconds after we polish it. We hear bloodcurdling screams in the night, but there's no one there." "All right, all right, I'm convinced something is happening," replied the preacher. "You and your wife stay in church all night tonight, and I'll stay in your house."

Armed with only his Bible, prayer book, and a large wooden cross, the preacher bravely made himself comfortable before the fire in the hearth. He didn't have to wait long. A small child, dead long enough that its decayed flesh was falling off its bones, appeared. "Do you fear Satan?" the corpse inquired. The preacher opened his prayer book and began to read aloud. The apparition dissolved in a luminous mist. Next came a huge writhing snake, its body covered in red and black scales, its eyes flashing fire, "You should fear evil," it hissed. The preacher struck it with his cross, and the serpent disappeared in a flash of fire, leaving only ashes. Next came the most fearsome apparitions: two great hounds, their lips bared around sharp teeth shining with a phosphorescent green glow, and sparks flying off their tangled black fur. "Prepare to meet Satan!" they snarled as they began their leap toward the preacher. Confidently, he held out his Bible in front of them. As the Hounds of Hell came into direct contact with the Holy Book, they recoiled, yelping in agony. Suddenly their bodies were enveloped in a searing white flame, and they were no more.

Exhausted, the preacher fell into a deep, untroubled sleep. When he awakened in the morning, the professor and his wife asked him what had happened. "I fell asleep and had the most terrifying nightmare," replied the preacher. "At least, I hope it was just a nightmare, but I think the forces of evil have left this house now." He was right.

The Phantom Disciplinarian

The school looks very ordinary. It stands on a whole block of land, including its blacktopped playground, in a part of Cincinnati that was built up mostly from the 1920s through the 1940s. The public elementary school is of a classic 1930s design, a three-story brown brick building trimmed with glazed terra cotta in yellow, green, and purple.

Inside, the floors are covered in worn brown linoleum tiles, and the hallway walls are of yellow glazed brick—nothing extraordinary. Graduates from long ago, returning as parents or grandparents attending school plays or basketball games, remark that the school not only looks the same as when they were pupils, but also smells the same—a mixture of dust, chalk, sweat, and disinfectant.

Many who work at the school—teachers, secretaries, janitors, and administrators—believe that something else hasn't changed either: the presence of Miss Brooks, a onetime teacher there who died twenty years ago. Miss Brooks was a strict disciplinarian. She would not tolerate misbehavior. Definitely "old school," she did not hesitate to pinch an errant student's arm or ear or smack a rear end to enforce the rules, which Miss Brooks held sacred. Her principal and fellow teachers loved her. Just a frowning glare from Miss Brooks could bring instant order and quiet to a roomful of restless kids. In these days when any corporal punishment, no matter how richly deserved, triggers lawsuits, Miss Brooks wouldn't get away with it. But dead people can't be sued, and ghosts care nothing about angry parents. Miss Brooks's spirit seems to have decided to stick around the school where she spent so much of her life, and she is still enforcing the rules her way.

No one has actually seen the ghost, but young lawbreakers claim to have felt her corrective smack or tweak. An unseen but definitely felt hand delivers a whack on the seat of pupils who talk when they shouldn't, harass other kids, or don't maintain a straight line during fire drills. To be fair, it must be noted that Miss Brooks's spirit can be very protective of students in real danger. One boy reported that as he was about to cross the busy street in front of the school, an unseen arm was flung across his chest just as a car ran a red light and surely would have killed him if he had not been restrained.

So behave! Stay in line! No talking! Obey the rules or risk the wrath of the ghost of the disciplinarian teacher.

Please, No! No!

This is a particularly horrifying ghost story because the circumstances that produced the ghost are so horrific in themselves. This pitiful little ghost is said to still haunt the scene of the shameful abuse and violence that led to the most untimely death of a child. The house in question is located in an aging but still respectable middle-class neighborhood of Cincinnati. No one stays in this house for more than a few months. Several owners have placed the property back on the market, selling at a loss, after encountering this ghost.

Usually, the phantom doesn't appear right away when the owners or tenants move in. Also, as seems to be typical of haunted houses, the family pets are the first to sense the supernatural presence, and the first to react to ghosts.

Several of those who have encountered this ghost report the same initial contact. At various times throughout the day, when the house is quiet, a young boy's voice is heard begging tearfully, "No, please, no!" This may be repeated several times before the voice fades away. An upper-floor bedroom appears to be the source of these plaintive cries, but an investigation reveals that no one is there.

Neighbors have reported seeing a pale, tear-stained little face staring out an upstairs window at times when no living child could have been in the house. The local legend is that this little ghost is the unhappy spirit of a boy who lived there more than forty years ago. The boy, about five or six years old, was left in the care of an uncle while his widowed mother went to work. It was feared by some in the neighborhood that the boy might be being sexually abused, but sadly, no one attempted to help him.

Finally, one day, the little boy is said to have died as a result of a fall down the steep steps between the first and second floors. Was it an accident, a murder, or a desperate suicide? No one will ever know what caused the death of the helpless, apparently terrified little boy, but no one who has lived in that house doubts the existence of his sad ghost.

The Trembling Spirits of Pleasant Run

Those who have witnessed the rare appearance of the spirits of Pleasant Run, in the northern suburbs of Cincinnati, find the experience somehow very disturbing. Not that these ghosts intend to frighten the living. Actually, they seem oblivious to the presence of the living and show no inclination to interact with them. It is the odd behavior of the ghosts, with as many as twenty or thirty spirits present at some manifestations, that onlookers find peculiar and rather unnerving.

These phantoms appear to be possessed by some powerful emotional force and follow a distinctly weird set of behaviors. First one or two of the ghosts fall into a kind of trance or state of suspended animation. Others then follow. Next, without warning, the ghosts begin to twitch, jerking their limbs about as though they were puppets on strings. Soon some are whirling in circles, faster and faster, with an unfocused stare from unseeing eyes, open-mouthed and moaning. A few may drop to all fours and begin barking like dogs.

Those unfortunate enough to have witnessed these eerie ghosts thought at the time that these hysterical happenings went on for hours, though only a few minutes actually had passed. It was as though the human witnesses to the ghostly appearances themselves were bewitched somehow. Just what is going on among the spirits in Pleasant Run?

Historians point to the fact that late in the year 1801, an eccentric religious sect called the New Lights arrived in Pleasant Run. They were part of a group of as many as three thousand people who customarily fell into deep trances, followed by erratic, frantic activity, during religious ceremonies. Outsiders considered the New Lights adherents to be crazy and sometimes visited their services in order to watch in amused fascination as though at a sideshow. The only problem was that sometimes those who came to scoff found themselves joining in with the mad jerking, twirling, and barking. So don't stop to stare too long at the New Lights ghosts, or you might begin to join their twitching dances of spiritual possession!

Imprisoned Ghosts

According to ghost hunters, old prisons usually are hot spots where supernatural manifestations are common and multiple ghosts have been seen for many decades. One of Ohio's chief hot spots is Ohio State Penitentiary, dating to 1834, with many additions and reconstructions since.

No one can be very surprised that prisons are filled not just with living prisoners, but with ghosts as well, for prisons are like deep wells of human misery and despair. Many a man and woman has died behind bars, bitter and forlorn, with a heart filled with hate and despair.

For many prisoners, violence sent them to prison, violence dogged their footsteps every day, and violence ended their lives behind prison walls. The Ohio State Penitentiary was the scene of one of America's worst prison disasters on April 21, 1930. An inside plot to engineer a mass escape included setting a small fire to divert the attention of guards. The trouble was, the small fire quickly became large and uncontrollable. A total of 322 men died, many of whom burned to death in their cells. Others, also locked securely away from any hope of escape into fresh air, died of smoke inhalation. The chaos of rioting during and after the fire led to a general lockdown, as the whole complex was placed under military control. It is said that prisoners' corpses lay in their cells rotting for more than a week before order finally was restored.

Perhaps not surprisingly, the most hideous ghosts said to haunt the state penitentiary are those victims of the great fire. Many have reported sightings of the "charred thirteen"—thirteen horrifyingly disfigured, burned bodies that haunt the site of the fire. The sight of them, with their charred flesh flaking off in black shreds, their carbonized hair still smoking, and their poached eyes staring blindly from lidless sockets, is bad enough. Even worse, report ghost hunters, is the suffocating stench of badly burned flesh. As ghost researchers recognize, odors are frequent accompaniments to ghostly sightings, and then there are the tortured screams and incessant moaning sounds of the long-suffering dead. Whatever their crimes, the eternal punishment of the charred thirteen seems harsh.

The Witches of Jackson

When folks move to a new home, far from their place of birth, they bring with them their familiar customs and beliefs, even their own tales of the supernatural. And so it was with a group of Welsh settlers whose arrival at Jackson in 1818 was entirely accidental. As the story goes, these Welsh emigrants were coming down the Ohio River, heading west, when fate changed their plans. They had tied up their boats at Gallipolis one night, to discover in the morning that their boats had been stolen, along with their tools and supplies intended to enable them to begin a new life farming in the West. The men subsequently found work building a road toward Chillicothe, and thus wound up in Jackson at a time when local coal mines were opening. Now, the Welsh know a thing or two about coal mining, and the men soon had jobs in the mines.

One of the mines was owned by a particularly nasty and stingy man, one John Bull. Bull drove his miners hard, insisting on long hours underground and cheating them on their pay. The Welshmen decided to use traditional Welsh witchcraft to teach John Bull a lesson he'd never forget. They determined to make a witch's bridle and have the oldest woman in their group use it to ride John Bull until he dropped of exhaustion.

In Welsh folklore, a witch's bridle is handwoven from hairs pulled from a horse's tail by the light of a full moon. The victim's name is used in a rhyme repeated three times at midnight. Thus, "John Bull, you'll rue this night; John Bull, you'll feel the witch's might."

The old woman, recently appointed community witch, took her bridle to John Bull's house one dreary midnight. A powerful wind suddenly arose, blowing open his locked door. The witch threw her horsehair bridle about his neck, commanding the terrified man to get down on all fours so she could ride him. Bull could not resist her supernatural powers and complied.

The story goes that the witch rode John Bull hard, through briers and brush all night. By morning, Bull agreed on fair wages and decent treatment of his Welsh miners, and he never dared go back on his word. It is said that long afterward, just the sight of a horsehair bridle would convince anyone in the neighborhood that fair dealing with the Welsh was a wise policy.

Why the Buzzards Keep Returning

Can animals possess some sort of mystical memory of times long past? Or can they have a special sensitivity to some supernatural qualities of a place, one to which they are drawn every year on the same date, as if by magic? These are good questions, which recur every year in the tiny town of Hinckley, about fifteen miles south of Cleveland.

Every year on March 15, infamous in ancient history as the Ides of March, when Julius Caesar was assassinated, the buzzards return to Hinckley. Similarly to the famous swallows of Capistrano, California, seventy or eighty or more buzzards return to Hinckley precisely on schedule. It is thought that these large scavengers spend the winter in the Smoky Mountains. But why do they come back to Hinckley like clockwork every year?

Vultures eat carrion, which is to say, they consume dead meat. They are nature's cleanup squad; circling overhead or perched high in trees, their ominous presence often signals the funeral of some poor creature.

One legend explaining the buzzards' arrival on March 15 of every year is that it's the anniversary of an event that provided an unforgettable bonanza of buzzard food. The story is that an obese woman of the Wyandot tribe, convicted of witchcraft, was hanged in Hinckley in 1808. This witch supposedly had been practicing the black arts for many years and proudly admitted being a loyal servant of Satan. She even claimed to have been Satan's sex toy, gleefully recounting the many obscene perversions in which she happily participated.

It is said that she laughed when sentenced to death for witchcraft. "My body will poison the soil for miles around my grave!" she promised. "No crops will grow, nor animals graze; no birds or game will fall to the hunter, no fish will be caught—this area will be cursed for nine generations." Outraged and fearful, the townspeople decided to deny the witch a burial, instead leaving her grossly fat body hanging from the gallows.

As the witch's body rotted, scores of huge buzzards gathered to feast on her. Was the corpse of a witch especially tasty? The buzzards seem to think so, and their descendants, still hopeful of another spicy meal, come back every March 15.

The Ghost in the Seamless Garment

Not that any ghost is routine or mundane, but this ghost really is different. It hasn't been seen much of late, but folks around Salesville used to see it, or so they said. The specter is a middle-aged man of no particular distinction. He appears to be wearing a long, flowing white robe, of which he seems to be unusually proud. He parades up and down like a fashion model, stopping to turn about to better display his twirling robe. Some observers claim that the phantom has a rather smug smile on his face, as though he'd finally achieved some special distinction or unusual triumph. If approached, the faintly glowing apparition simply evaporates like early-morning fog when the sun rises.

Just who is, or was, this mysterious "clothes horse," as old-timers would have called him? Local tradition has it that this is the ghost of one Joseph Dylkes, who once lived hereabouts. Dylkes was a rather ordinary man who distinguished himself by one day standing up in church meeting to make an important announcement. "I am God!" he said, with appropriate drama. Some of those present, being of suspicious mind, wondered out loud if Joseph had drunk too freely of the excellent Pennsylvania whiskey that was a common cargo along the nearby National Road, which at the time (1828) was the busiest highway in the nation. Others in the congregation were silently skeptical of this astounding claim, while a few took Joe at his word and attached themselves to him as apostles.

As time went on, the community's unbelievers, and even a few believers, suggested that Joseph Dylkes prove his divinity by working a miracle or two. Dylkes duly announced that he would appear in a seamless garment, a traditional symbol of earthly perfection. This impending miracle was well advertised, and crowds began to gather at Dylkes's public appearances.

Alas, the seamless garment never appeared. Joe and his dwindling group of disciples chose to seek the New Jerusalem elsewhere and wandered away. Years later, a few onetime converts returned to Salesville and reported that Dylkes had disappeared "somewhere in Philadelphia." Evidently, no Philadelphians missed him, and the mystery was never solved.

Is his ghost now wearing a truly seamless garment? No one yet has gotten close enough to inspect his ghostly robe. Perhaps you shouldn't try either.

The Spying Spaceships

The area around Dayton seems to be a hot spot for supposed sightings of alien spacecraft or unidentified flying objects. These encounters, reported by many over the years, appear to have an obvious explanation—the area's association with aeronautical research and development. There are two schools of thought on this hyperactivity of UFOs around Dayton. One is that the UFOs are supersecret government experimental craft being developed at the Air Force's Wright-Patterson Field. The second, perhaps more generally believed theory is that alien spacecraft frequent the area, out of curiosity about earthlings' progress in aeronautical research.

The states of Ohio and North Carolina both boast about being "first in flight" because of the Wright Brothers' success in developing the first flight by a heavier-than-air craft. Ohio has the stronger case, as Dayton, the brothers' hometown, was the site of the extensive and secretive research and experimentation that led to that first successful flight. At the time, in the early years of the twentieth century, there was a great deal of intense rivalry among inventors trying to produce the first true airplane. Wilbur and Orville Wright were not mere lucky tinkerers; they were persistent experimenters. They built the world's first wind tunnel at Dayton to test wing design.

The reason the Wrights traveled to North Carolina's Outer Banks to field-test their first airplane was not just because Kitty Hawk was windy and flat. It was to minimize the chances of being watched by strangers. Real strange observers—from outer space. The brothers long had had an uneasy feeling that their experiments with kites, gliders, and wing designs were being watched, and not just by competitors. Logically, if earth were being observed by visiting aliens from outer space, they would have a keen interest in our planet's progress with airplanes. The skies over Dayton were reportedly frequented by UFOs long before there was a name for them. The story of a family we'll call the Beams is typical of the many encounters with UFOs experienced by folks in the Dayton area.

It happened on July 4, 1918, as recorded in family tradition, handed down over the generations. The Wrights had continued their research on bigger, better, and faster aircraft ever since that fateful first flight in 1903. New aircraft designs constantly were being tested over Dayton, where the brothers were manufacturing large numbers of planes. The Wright airplane company shipped more than forty-five hundred military airplanes to France during World War I, so Dayton was the air capital of the world at the time.

The Beam family lived on a farm on the outskirts of Dayton, not far from the Huffman Prairie Flying Field, scene of the Wright Brothers' secret experiments, now part of the huge Wright-Patterson Air Force Base. The family decided on a backyard picnic in order to view the fireworks display planned yearly.

Just at dusk, before the fireworks got under way, they were amazed by what they saw overhead. An enormous, cigar-shaped craft appeared suddenly. It hovered overhead for twenty minutes or

so, making no sound and displaying no lights. Could it be a dirigible, like the Germans' zeppelins? But then the strange craft abruptly flew away at an impossible speed for a dirigible. Had the Beams seen a secret Wright Brothers or Army experiment? Patriotically, they agreed not to talk about it outside the family. Only when their grandchildren heard this family story did anyone wonder whether they had been visited by a UFO intent on spying on American aeronautical research. Now, we will never know exactly what mysterious craft flew over Dayton in 1918, or since, but the stories continue from many sources.

The Spirited Sisters

The tiny town of Homer, northwest of Columbus, apparently hosts two rather flamboyant and rambunctious ghosts, the shades of two sisters born here but buried far away in England. In life, Victoria Claflin Woodhull and Tennessee "Tennie" Claflin were very controversial characters. People at the time referred to them as free spirits, and that is exactly what they are in death too.

For most people, ghostly apparitions are not a welcome sight. Most of us would just as soon not encounter spirits, but the ghosts of the Claflin sisters might be an exception. These phosphorescent spirits appear late on moonless nights, dancing and merrily cavorting, and they are nude—and, according to male observers, pretty good-looking. Interested?

As young girls, Vicky and Tennie began giving spiritualistic sessions to neighbors and townspeople. For a fee, they would call up the shades of deceased loved ones and pass messages between the spirit world and that of the living. Each had married, divorced, and remarried and divorced again before their ambitions took them to New York City. This move may have been prompted when their father was run out of town on suspicion of arson for profit. Financial chicanery may have run in the family, according to contemporaries.

Vicky and Tennie set themselves as spiritualist advisors to the wealthy and powerful in New York. They gained the confidence of millionaire Cornelius Vanderbilt, who, they said, gave them financial tips on the stock market.

Exactly what services the sisters provided to Vanderbilt and his rich friends is not clear, but soon they too were rich. The Claflin girls set up a combination brokerage office and free love clinic, which was patronized by New York's wealthy investors. The "free" in free love referred to the uninhibited nature of services provided, not the absence of cost. The lovely sisters grew richer and richer, with a client list of some five hundred happy customers.

Vicky and Tennie launched a new women's magazine in which they advocated women's rights, female suffrage, and free abortions, which were not particularly popular views at the time. Vicky ran for president in 1872 on the Equal Rights ticket and campaigned vigorously, if futilely.

When Cornelius Vanderbilt died in 1877, his will allotted a great deal of money to Vicky and Tennie to finance their continuing research on spiritualism, and also possibly to ensure their silence about their free love clinic. Vanderbilt's children contested the will, and the sisters accepted a settlement, then sailed for England. There they each married into the aristocracy and lived happily ever after.

But their spirits still like to shock folks back in Homer by dancing in the nude and enjoying the reactions of their outraged former neighbors. Vicky and Tennie always were free spirits. And they really are cute.

Plain City's Phantom Pilgrims

A strange-looking group of about forty men, women, and children, all dressed alike in an odd tunic-style garment, wander along the banks of a little creek in the town of Plain City, a few miles west of Columbus. Their drab canvas tunics are filthy, their hands and faces are crusted with dirt, and their long, lank hair hangs in greasy, tangled curls. They wear only crude sandals on their dirty feet. They look as though they would smell bad, but most observers couldn't detect an odor, for these disheveled specters are only ghosts, mere wisps of fog that disappear if approached by the living. Some claim that the little ragtag band is distinguished by all of its members holding begging bowls in outstretched hands. This detail reinforces the belief that these are the ghosts of the Wandering Pilgrims, a religious sect that showed up in Plain City during the winter of 1816–17.

There seemed to be a number of exotic religious groups prowling about the frontier in those days. The Wandering Pilgrims stuck out as really different, though, as they thought of themselves as holy beggars, expecting others to feed them as they devoted their days not to productive work, but to contemplation of the life of the spirit. Aside from their persistent begging for food from their hardworking neighbors, the Wandering Pilgrims' belief in not washing their bodies or their clothing did not endear them to the townspeople. They also did not believe in using forks, spoons, or plates when eating.

The pilgrims' leader, known only by the title of prophet, apparently decided to impress the skeptical community with the holiness of his scruffy little band, and perhaps encourage more generous donations, by performing a miracle. He would, he announced, walk on water to celebrate Easter. This event was to take place on a nearby stream. The story is that some cynical boys from town suspected a trick and investigated the locale of the announced miracle, finding a plank walkway cleverly constructed a few inches beneath the surface. They secretly removed a few planks. The prophet confidently set out on his miraculous walk on water and suddenly disappeared from sight, much to the consternation of his flock and the delight of the skeptics.

The pilgrims decided to wander elsewhere after that, but their ghosts still stroll by sometimes, holding their begging bowls hopefully. But no one now makes a donation, so they soon fade away.

The Gutless Ghost

Just west of Cincinnati in the town of Addyston is an imposing monument to William Henry Harrison, war hero and the first Ohioan to become president of the United States. Only two hundred feet to the west lies the grave of William's only son to reach adulthood, John Scott Harrison, and this site reportedly is haunted by his truly gruesome ghost.

The ghost of John Scott Harrison doesn't appear as often as it once did, which may be just as well for the mental health of passersby. This ghost is as unique in his appearance as in his personal history. He is a slightly phosphorescent spirit seen sitting atop his tombstone, alert and aggressively staring at any who approach. He holds a large revolver in his right hand, but what makes this ghost really different is that only his head and limbs are intact. His chest is empty, the ribs torn open. His torso is missing, with only his spine visible where his abdomen should be, thus earning this spirit the nickname "Gutless Ghost." There is an interesting story behind this phantom's missing body parts and his brandishing a gun.

President William Henry Harrison, who died after only thirty days in office, fathered ten children, only one of whom, John Scott, outlived him. John served two terms in Congress but spent most of his life as a successful farmer. His major claim to fame is that he is the only son of a president to have fathered a president, Benjamin Harrison.

John Scott Harrison was buried practically in the shadow of his famous father's tomb in 1878, but he didn't stay there, literally. His son Benjamin was tipped off that his father's body had been stolen by grave robbers and sold to the Cincinnati Medical School. The future president, furious at this indignity to his father, stormed into the school and discovered his father's partially disemboweled corpse hidden in a dumbwaiter. There was no way to identify his father's organs, now scattered among other medical specimens, so what was left of John Scott was placed back in his coffin for reburial. That night, the story goes, his ghost appeared to his son suggesting that a loaded revolver be placed in the coffin as a symbol of his spirit's determination to stay in his grave. Benjamin accordingly put a Colt .38 in the coffin. So beware the Gutless Ghost—he may be gutless in the physical sense, but not in the emotional sense.

The Compulsive Butler

For obvious reasons, the current owners of this property do not wish it to be identified. The huge stone house was built in the 1890s on a broad avenue heading north from Cincinnati's city center. Set within spacious grounds, now converted to provide ample parking spaces, the ornate mansion features large downstairs rooms paneled in golden oak, with Indiana limestone fireplaces and leaded stained-glass windows. Anyone with enough money to maintain it evidently would prefer less ostentatious, more modern luxury, so the grand old place has become a funeral parlor, and a prestigious one at that. It is haunted, not by the recently deceased whose coffins lie briefly in its spacious rooms, but by a onetime butler in the house who just won't leave—at least, according to current employees who must work though the night, preparing the dead and cleaning and maintaining the old mansion.

The realization that the house is haunted by a former butler is based on two sets of observations. The most compelling evidence is the common occurrence of objects being moved about when no one is in the room. There is, however, no similarity here to the well-known poltergeist phenomenon. Poltergeists intend to harass and frighten people by causing objects to move, often smashing dishes or decorative items. In this house, however, objects are carefully restored to their proper places as determined by the mostly unseen spirit.

The new owners and their staff soon realized that if they moved an object such as a vase from its customary position, it would mysteriously move back. Once they deemed a display of wax flowers under a large glass dome too old-fashioned and removed it from a living-room table to an upstairs closet. The next morning, it was back in place. The staff noticed that brass doorknobs and fireplace fenders, along with silver candelabra and vases, never needed polishing, at least not by human hands. Mirrors and windows always gleamed as though freshly cleaned.

Then there were rare, fleeting glimpses of a distinguished-looking elderly gentleman dressed formally in old-fashioned butler's garb—black trousers and tailcoat, gray vest, and black tie. Had some long-ago butler in the household come from the dead to keep the house as immaculate as during his lifetime?

Some staff argued for obtaining the services of professional ghost hunters, but the present owner refused. The volunteer phantom butler, he reasoned, was an asset, not a problem. The compulsively neat spirit didn't require a pension or a dental plan, much less paychecks. The ghost butler never appeared during regular business hours or tried to frighten anyone. So it was decided to let the ghost go about his self-assigned chores and stay out of his way. Oh, and don't move anything from its proper place.

The Protective She-Wolf

Some Cincinnatians swear that the wolf has stared them down with its fiercely glowing yellow eyes if they should get a little too close to her, especially during the evening. She will even growl threateningly if she senses any threat to the young ones nursing at her nipples. Not that such protective behavior would be unexpected in a nursing she-wolf; what makes it unusual is that the wolf and her young are stone. Further, her hungry little dependents are depicted not as wolf cubs, but as human babies.

The Capitoline wolf statue, a famous landmark in Cincinnati's Eden Park, was a long-ago gift to the city's Italian-American community from Benito Mussolini, onetime dictator of Italy. The beautifully carved statue is meant to tell the story of the mythical she-wolf that was said to have mothered, fed, and protected the infant twins Romulus and Remus, who grew up to become the founders of the city of Rome. To this day, a caged wolf is kept on display on Rome's Capitoline Hill as a reminder of the mythical founding of the city.

Is Cincinnati's copy of the Capitoline wolf statue bewitched? Does it really growl on occasion, or is that motherly protective gesture merely an illusion?

Desolation

It is entirely appropriate that Dayton, Wilbur and Orville Wright's hometown, should be the site of the national museum of the U.S. Air Force. The museum's Presidential Aircraft Gallery enables tourists to visit the aircraft that served Presidents Franklin Roosevelt, Harry Truman, John F. Kennedy, and Lyndon Johnson. This particular Air Force One, a Boeing 707, holds a unique position within the presidential lineup, for it was the scene of the swearing in of the new president, Johnson, following the brutal assassination of his predecessor, Kennedy, whose corpse then was carried back to Washington in the rear compartment. Some believe that this aircraft is haunted, though the ghost's appearances are not widely known because most witnesses feel protective of this tragic spirit.

Only a handful have observed the phantom of a lady, for she seems to possess the reserved dignity so characteristic of the living person. The very few willing to admit to seeing this spirit say that she appears only briefly as a barely visible, faintly shimmering mist. Her grief is so overwhelmingly evident in her dejected posture, downcast eyes, and utterly desolate expression that observers instinctively look away in profound sympathy. Why this particular venue for this ghost? Perhaps it was only back on Air Force One that the full emotional impact of what had happened that day was able to break through the stunned disbelief that afflicts eyewitnesses to horror. This spirit seems to personify the desolation of those suddenly bereaved by senseless violence.

Distress Sign

There is a type of apparition that students of the supernatural refer to as guardian spirits. These are the ghosts of those truly dedicated souls who, in a sense, are still on duty after death. Many were, in life, military personnel, police officers, and others similarly sworn to protect and serve.

One guardian spirit is that of a former Cincinnati fire department captain whose phantom appears in dire emergencies, when fire threatens lives as well as property, and seconds count in preventing disaster. What distinguishes the captain's silent warnings to his fellow firefighters is that his ghost gives the ancient distress sign of the Masons, the fraternity in which he was a longtime and dedicated member. It is said that in Masonic tradition, the secret sign by which members ask their brethren for help is to be used only in the most serious circumstances. When the captain was on active duty more than four decades ago, he could count on a high proportion of fellow Masons among his colleagues. He knew that using the Masonic distress sign would serve to underline and emphasize the urgency of its early warning.

In fire stations across Cincinnati, the appearance of the captain's ghost, in his ceremonial parade uniform and flashing an unusual sign, alerts everyone that very shortly the official notification of a fire emergency will reach them. Forewarned, the firefighters thus are able to shave vital seconds from their reaction time. The captain is still on duty!

Whoa!

Just to the west of downtown Springfield sits a beautifully restored relic of the past, the Pennsylvania House. Built around 1840, this roadside inn and tavern once was famous as the "Inn at the End of the National Road." It now is a museum operated by the Daughters of the American Revolution, and according to some, it is haunted. Or at least the inn's yard, once filled with Conestoga wagons and still a parking lot for visitors, is haunted.

It happens late at night, long after the museum closes. The neighborhood is largely made up of industries and warehouses, very quiet at night. Phantom wagons, covered with white canvas and drawn by six horses to haul their heavy freight loads up steep slopes, have been seen slowly lumbering along the old National Road, now U.S. 40. The National Road was the first long-distance highway authorized by Congress. The section from Cumberland, Maryland, to Wheeling, West Virginia, was completed by 1818, but the road didn't reach Springfield until 1838. The road was a very busy one, bringing many pioneers into the Midwest in wagons and stagecoaches, until at last it was outmoded by railroads. The wagons were manned by a rugged, no-nonsense, hard-driving, and hard-swearing brotherhood known as teamsters, because they drove teams of horses, mules, or oxen.

For these teamsters, a night at the Pennsylvania House, with a few drinks, a meal, a few more drinks, some card playing, a few more drinks, and a bed for the night, was their reward for a long, tough haul over the National Road. Their ghostly shouts of "Whoa!" still echo as the phantom wagons pull up to the Pennsylvania House's broad porch. Rest at last for the exhausted spirits of men and beasts.

Marmalade Knows

Marmalade knows—he really knows, and that is the scary part, for what he knows is when someone is soon to be visited by the Angel of Death. Marmalade's eerie foreknowledge, furthermore, did not end with his own death, for Marmalade's ghost continues to possess the awesome ability to identify impending death.

Marmalade was a large, somewhat independent, and aloof tomcat. His ghost has the same personality, as well as his apparently supernatural awareness of when death awaits. He got his name because his owner, a medical doctor and hospital administrator, thought that the cat's striped orange fur resembled English-cut orange marmalade, a favorite treat of hers.

The story of Marmalade was told by his former owner on the grounds of anonymity for both the person and the hospital where the cat's premonitions first came to light. It can be revealed that the hospital, now closed and abandoned, was in a poverty-stricken neighborhood of Cincinnati.

The doctor, whom we'll call Dr. Ellen Hartly, was walking to her car one evening when she heard a faint, plaintive meowing coming from a trash can in an alley near the hospital. Investigating the sound, she found that a tiny kitten had been thrown away. She took the starving fur ball home and gave it food, love, and a name. The kitten became strongly attached to his savior, so much so that the good doctor couldn't bear his pathetic clinging to her, fearful of abandonment again. So Marmalade went to the doctor's hospital office with her daily. At first happy to doze on the carpet while the doctor went about her administrative chores, the growing kitten began to roam the hallways, tagging along with doctors and nurses as they made their rounds.

As Marmalade matured, he became a very self-contained cat, affectionate only toward his rescuer, but mostly ignoring the rest of the human race. He did not respond well to strangers, with one notable exception: On occasion, for no apparent reason, he would jump up on a patient's bed and shower the person with attention and affection. Though others might receive a nasty scratch from being too bold in petting Sir Marmalade, a select few were favored by an atypically friendly visit.

Gradually rumors spread that Marmalade's attention was directed only to patients who were about to die. It was unsettling to realize that the cat was attempting, in his own feline way, to comfort those soon to depart this world for the one of spirits.

Marmalade lost his life in the hospital parking lot when a recklessly moving car quickly hit him, narrowly missing his owner. Shortly afterward, nurses and doctors began to catch fleeting glimpses of the cat's spirit still making his rounds. And just as before, curling up on the beds of those about to die, Marmalade's ghost was carrying on the living cat's mission to bring warm attention and comfort to the dying.

The really scary part of Marmalade's story is that similar stories have come to light elsewhere. Are cats just hypersensitive to human frailty as life begins to flicker out? In the witch-hunting craze of centuries past, people suspected cats of having supernatural powers. Do they really? Only the cats know for sure.

The Long-Winded Grace

In and around the city of Mansfield, a guest preacher has been known to show up to fill in when regular clergy cannot appear as a result of sudden illness or unanticipated family problems. This timely volunteer is dressed simply in a black suit of an old-fashioned cut, and he wears a string tie of the sort popular just before the Civil War.

Somehow this guest preacher has sensed the need for a replacement minister, as it turns out that in the confusion of an emergency surrounding the usual spiritual leader, no one actually sent for a last-minute substitute. The preacher just came, and just in time. If there is any complaint from his temporary flock, it is that the guest was rather long-winded, often setting records for the length of his earnest but interminable sermons.

It is only after his departure that some in the congregation suspect that they've seen a ghost. They have, for they've witnessed one of John Finney's occasional materializations from the spirit realm, as Finney is long dead.

The story is that John Finney, a farmer, sincere Christian, and lay preacher in his church, was active in the Underground Railroad, which assisted runaway slaves fleeing to safe sanctuary in Canada. Ohio, a free state bordering on the Southern slave states, contained many ardent antislavery citizens who participated in the secret system of safe houses (known as stations) and guides (conductors).

John Finney was a station agent, or safe house manager. He would hide and feed runaways on his farm until they could join a "train" at night, heading for a boat across Lake Erie to freedom. Not all Ohioans agreed with the abolitionists who insisted on defying federal law, as the Fugitive Slave Act had made it a crime to aid runaways, and during the War of 1812, the British spread rumors that escaped slaves would be paid a bounty to kill white Americans.

Early one morning, a mob descended on John Finney's farm, demanding that the well-known abolitionist and suspected member of the Underground Railroad surrender the slaves they'd heard he was hiding. "Where is your warrant?" inquired Finney. "Law-abiding citizens would have a warrant." The invaders agreed to send one of their number to the courthouse for a warrant. Concerned that his unwelcome visitors would wander about and discover the fugitives, Finney invited them all into his kitchen to join him for breakfast. The would-be slave catchers, seduced by the aroma of frying bacon and eggs, gathered around the table. "You are all God-fearing churchgoers, aren't you?" inquired Finney of his hypocritical breakfast guests. "Let us say grace." Finney then launched into the longest, most fervent, most eloquent prayer ever heard in Ohio. The runaways had ample time to disappear over the horizon by the time Finney wound down and his guests could eat breakfast. For decades afterward, any exceptionally long-winded prayer, grace, or sermon was known as a "Finney."

Should you by chance be regaled by an unexpected guest sermon that seems endless, take note. You just might be listening to a well-intentioned but very verbose ghost.

Columbus
and the Western Heartland

THE BUCKEYE STATE'S WESTERN HEARTLAND REGION ENCOMPASSES the western half of the area south of the Lakeshore, north of the Ohio Valley, and excluding the Cincinnati-Dayton complex of the Southwest. The Western Heartland includes Ohio's capital and largest city, Columbus, as well as Lancaster, Chillicothe, Marion, Lima, and Bowling Green. In this large region can be found legends of swamp monsters and ghosts from the Indian wars and the Civil War. There are unusual stories surrounding the mysterious Great Serpent Mound. The Devil makes a cameo appearance in one old tale, and you'll encounter a possible witch or two, including the only first lady ever accused of murdering her husband.

Swamp Monsters

Monsters once terrorized anyone brave enough to enter the fearsome Black Swamp of northwestern Ohio. The Black Swamp once stretched for many miles along the valley of the Maumee River, from Antwerp through Defiance and Napoleon to Perrysburg near Toledo.

This northwestern corner of Ohio was the last part of the state to be settled, and for good reason. It was a desolate, forbidden land, avoided by early settlers. Early travelers told of wading in water up to their hips as they struggled through dense timber. The huge trees blocked out most of the sunlight at the surface, hence the name Black Swamp. The standing water ruled out any thoughts of clearing the land for farming. Bears roamed the dark swamplands, and rattlesnakes and copperheads added to the danger.

But the real terrors of the Black Swamp were mysterious creatures known only as Swamp Monsters. Only the vaguest, most general descriptions of this horror exist. This was before the advent of cameras, and evidently anyone who got close enough to a Swamp Monster to provide a detailed description did not survive the encounter. Survivors of long-distance sightings of the creatures could only agree that the monster appeared to walk upright, at least some of the time, and could move very quickly. A few observers claimed that it also could run on all fours. It appeared to be covered in long black hair or fur, and everyone agreed that it seemed to give off a powerful and disagreeable odor. Some eyewitnesses claimed that the creature stood at least six feet tall. The Swamp Monster seemed to prefer avoiding humans, as it moved quickly out of sight when confronted by two or more people. The creature could be spotted hiding among the trees as people moved about. Was it hiding from them or stalking them?

The bodies discovered after supposed encounters with Swamp Monsters were badly mauled, as though by sharp claws or teeth or both. Commonly, the victim's abdomen was torn open and its liver missing. Likewise, deer carcasses found in the Black Swamp were also mutilated in that fashion.

There was much speculation at the time as to the identity of the Swamp Monster. Could it be simply a large bear? Bears are known to rear up on their hind legs to search for prey and to frighten away any threat to themselves or their cubs. Bears also could fit the black fur part of the description. But the local Indians, who routinely hunted bears for fur and meat, also avoided the Black Swamp and told stories about "swamp men," whom they feared more than any animal predators. Were the Swamp Monsters some sort of primitive man or ape species?

Today most of the dreaded Black Swamp is history, having been drained by the middle of the nineteenth century so that farmers could grow crops in its rich, black muck. No one has seen Swamp Monsters for decades, so we don't have to worry. Or do we?

Awakening the Spirits of the Serpents

Traditionally, it happens every year on the spring equinox, the first day of spring on the astronomical calendar. The ancient Native American cultures calculated and celebrated the four cardinal events in earth-sun relationships—the two equinoxes and the two solstices. There is some evidence of Stonehenge-like arrangements of stones or wooden stakes, which enabled ancient peoples to track the changing sun angles related to the seasons.

At sunrise on the spring equinox, the sound of phantom drums sometimes can be heard faintly over Serpent Mound, the largest effigy mound in America, located near Hillsboro. In contrast to scores of conical mounds found throughout Ohio, effigy mounds are three-dimensional representations of living creatures made of earth and stone created long ago by Native Americans. The Great Serpent Mound, built of stone and yellow clay, depicts an enormous snake 1,330 feet long atop its writhing crest. The snake is 20 feet wide at its base and varies from 2 to 3½ feet tall. Most likely it once was much taller, having been subject to natural erosion over the centuries. This serpent consists of three horseshoe loops, with its tail ending in three close coils. The huge head of this snake appears about to swallow a massive egg-shaped mound, 30 by 80 feet at the base.

Many speculate that the ancients who created the Serpent Mound may have used it for religious ceremonies. It is known that Native Americans in this area were in awe of snakes, especially rattlesnakes, which held the power of sudden death in their fangs. Rattlesnakes hibernate through cold winters, being cold-blooded creatures. The increasing length of daylight and warmer sun of spring bring forth the formerly sluggish snakes, approximately around the time of the spring equinox.

Did early Native Americans celebrate the renewal of life—symbolized by the reemergence of snakes—at the Great Serpent Mound? Do the supernatural sounds of drums echo an ancient Indian seasonal celebration? And is it true that sunrise on the spring equinox creates an optical illusion of a writhing snake as light first strikes the top of the long, sinuous ridge of earth?

See for yourself some spring, and listen for the ghostly drums at dawn over Serpent Mound. But watch out for snakes awakened from their winter sleep by the mysterious throbbing drums.

Pursued by a UFO

The frequency with which UFOs are seen flying over the Great Serpent Mound is a mystery on top of a mystery. No one knows the reason for these overflights, and no one knows for sure why the huge effigy mound, the largest in America, was built in the first place, though it may have had religious functions. If so, does a spiritual power still concentrate there and somehow signal to UFOs? Or do UFOs use the snake-shaped mound for navigational purposes?

Though the reason for the attraction is uncertain, the frequency of UFO flyovers is well known to UFOlogists. People in the largely rural area near Hillsboro have become almost used to seeing mysterious lights late at night in the sky over the great mound. In one recent instance, a local woman returning from an evening shopping trip spotted a strange oval-shaped, silver craft with red lights running around its base, hovering over the Serpent Mound. Curious, she drove closer to the UFO, but then her engine stopped and would not start again for about twenty minutes. The strange craft drifted slowly over her vehicle, hovered for a few minutes, then suddenly accelerated vertically, rising to several thousand feet above her. After she successfully restarted the car and headed for home, she soon realized that the UFO was shadowing her, following from its great height.

When she pulled into her driveway and stopped, the odd craft descended to about fifty feet above, paused as though inspecting her, and then quickly flew south and out of sight. Thoroughly spooked, the woman decided to stay clear of UFOs in the future. Perhaps her obvious curiosity about it was returned by the occupants' curiosity about her.

The Witch of Marion

Was President Warren G. Harding's first lady really a witch? When Florence Kling Harding was alive, some of her contemporaries said that she acted like a witch, although first ladies tend to attract criticism, fair or not. Mrs. Harding's postmortem reputation as a witch may be similarly undeserved. At most, the reported actions of her spirit could just be due to a widow's anger at criticism of her husband, of whom she was very protective.

In life, Florence Harding was a bundle of contradictions. She was born to a successful business entrepreneur who provided middle-class comforts but tried to control his strong-willed daughter. At the age of nineteen, the future first lady ran away with a neighborhood boy, Henry DeWolfe, who turned out to be an abusive alcoholic. He fathered a son, Eugene, and then disappeared from Florence's life. She claimed to have divorced DeWolfe, but no record of either a marriage or a divorce exists.

Whatever else one might think of her, no one could doubt Florence Harding's determination or her ambition for her husband. Photographs of her as first lady show a steely-eyed woman with a more aggressive jaw than J. Edgar Hoover. She said, "I have only one real hobby—my husband!" and is quoted as telling him, "Well, Warren, I have got you the presidency; what are you going to do with it?"

Despite a chronic kidney ailment, Mrs. Harding entertained extensively, as her position required, even serving illegal alcohol to her husband's buddies. She was with her husband when he died in San Francisco following an exhausting tour of Alaska. Such was her reputation as the ruthless power behind the president that she was accused of poisoning him. Her motive purportedly was to spare him the indignity of being questioned in the developing scandals about to engulf his administration. The president's sudden death was somewhat mysterious; it didn't help that his widow absolutely forbade an autopsy.

Florence Harding died a year after her husband, but her story doesn't end with death. Some claim to have seen her stern face staring out the windows of her home-turned-museum in Marion, late at night when the house is closed, locked, and supposedly empty. Florence's spirit may be as fiercely protective of her husband's reputation now as she was in life.

Visitors to the Harding home may, if they express negative comments about America's twenty-ninth president, feel a painful rap on an elbow or knee. Unkind words about Warren Harding can mysteriously lead to a stumble on the porch steps or a flat tire in the parking lot. One tourist even claimed that his new car was deliberately scratched in the parking area behind the house after he made crude jokes about President Harding's well-known fathering of an illegitimate daughter. Is the unseen hand of Florence Kling Harding still at her home, continuing to defend the president's reputation? Some believe so, but that hardly makes her a witch, does it?

The Free Spirit

J. N. Free, both as a living man and as a ghost, truly was, and is, a free spirit. He was a well-known eccentric, which is to say that he was, in a perfectly harmless and even entertaining way, insane.

For family reasons, J. N. Free particularly liked the little city of Tiffin and made it his base, although he preferred to travel almost constantly. Free was born in Pennsylvania in 1828 but spent his boyhood on a farm near Tiffin. He studied law, preparing for a career as a lawyer, but like many other adventurous young men at the time, he joined the gold rush to California. There he made a fortune but was tricked out of it by clever crooks. He became seriously ill in mind and body, and even though he recovered his physical health, it became clear that his mind remained shattered.

Free decided to travel for the rest of his life, always going first class on trains and ships, and always patronizing the finest hotels and restaurants. But he never paid for anything. His delusion was that everyone was so glad of his company that he would be their gracious and entertaining guest. He could converse on any subject, was well read and well traveled, and had a large supply of wonderful stories. His eccentricities became his asset. "I am the immortal J. N.," he would announce as he waved away anyone so uncouth as to attempt to hand him a bill or ask to see his ticket or his money.

J. N. Free's story is amazingly similar to that of a similarly deluded San Franciscan who called himself Norton the First, Emperor of the United States and Protector of Mexico. Like Free, Norton had suffered a nervous breakdown after losing his fortune. As emperor, it was expected that his subjects would provide him with free meals, lodging, clothing, and transportation, and San Franciscans in the late nineteenth century gladly obliged their "emperor." J. N. Free was so popular and colorful a character that he attracted business to any hotel or restaurant that hosted him. Appreciative crowds would gather to be entertained by his stories. Sympathetic railroad executives gave him lifetime free passes rather than see him humiliated by being thrown off trains for nonpayment.

Why was there a community consensus to give J. N. a literal free ride in life? Many societies around the world have protected and indulged harmless eccentrics, believing that they possessed unique wisdom or philosophical insight. Medieval kings kept similarly delusionary individuals at court as storytellers, and some Indian tribes considered the nonaggressive mentally ill as being especially close to God and deserving of protection.

For decades after his death in 1906, the ghost of J. N. Free is said to have appeared in hotel lobbies, bars, and restaurants, beautifully dressed, very polite and friendly, and never reaching for the bill. In death, J. N. was as charming and harmless as he had been in life. There are those who claim that to this day, in the best restaurants and bars in Ohio's cities, a friendly and outgoing gentleman dressed in old-fashioned elegance entertains with his quick wit and great stories. At evening's end, he simply evaporates, leaving the bill for others to pay, which they do, grateful for a fascinating experience.

The Wicked Witch of Westerville

No one could figure out just how old Joann Robertson did it. She never seemed to work at anything, yet her farm prospered. Her cattle were always fat and healthy, her corn crop set records every year in both yield per acre and quality, and her house, barn, and fences always gleamed with fresh paint. Neat stacks of firewood stood beside her backdoor, though Joann never picked up an ax. Her windows sparkled, though Joann never was seen cleaning them. Just who was doing all the necessary work on the lonely old woman's farm?

Something odd was going on, that was for sure. Weird sounds and strange lights were heard and seen late at night on Joann's property. The neighbors avoided her farm at all times, but especially at night. Horses would balk at using the road past Joann's at night.

Hunting dogs refused to pursue game into the woods behind her house. Vicious black tomcats seemed to patrol her property lines, growling ferociously at any approaching strangers, man or beast.

Finally some local teenage boys, emboldened by a few beers, decided to investigate late one night. They climbed the rail fence around Joann's cornfield and stealthily crept toward her house. Suddenly a huge black coach appeared in the driveway. Drawn by four black horses breathing fire and striking sparks with their hooves on the stony ground, the coach drew up to Joann's front door. The coachman, dressed in scarlet, had horns atop his head and a long, forked tail. It was Satan in person! The boys hid, trembling, behind some barrels.

Throwing open the door of the satanic coach, the Devil declared, "Out! Get to work! Quickly now." As the boys watched in fascinated horror, the coach's wretched passengers stumbled out. The boys recognized many of them—neighborhood men and women whose sins were known widely, or at least suspected. Drunks, wife beaters, thieves, women of easy virtue—all began doing farm and household chores, working feverishly under the lash of a horsewhip wielded by Satan himself. "Work harder, faster, you miserable sinners!" snarled the Prince of Darkness. "Your sins have made you my slaves." The wicked witch Joann, transformed into a beautiful seductress, then led her evil master into the bedroom for a few lustful hours while the bewitched slaves went to work.

Witnessing the misery of the bewitched sinners, enslaved by their own unrepented sins, was a life-altering experience for the teens. It is said that their behavior became near angelic, and their church attendance much improved.

There is an obvious moral to this story: Unrepentant sinners will find themselves working like the devil for the Devil, or his minions. And be very careful if you venture onto a witch's property at night.

The Gray Ghosts of Camp Chase

What color are ghosts? In popular culture, spirits commonly are depicted as being white, as in a mist or fog. Some who have encountered ghosts were too terrified to remember whether the spirits appeared in full color or as white or light gray images. In the case of the spirits of Camp Chase Cemetery, the ghosts definitely are gray, as in Confederate Army gray, for these are the spirits of Confederate prisoners of war.

The largest prisoner-of-war camp operated by Union forces during the Civil War was at Columbus. Camp Chase, as it was known, lay west of downtown and across the Scioto River. Tourists today can find the cemetery that served Camp Chase just off Sullivan Avenue. The camp itself is history, but the cemetery remains as a known hot spot for supernatural occurrences.

An astonishing 2,260 Confederates are buried here, and many do not rest easy in their grave. Many of the men in gray are very bitter about their experience as prisoners of war, and justifiably so.

Nations at war sometimes agree to exchange prisoners of war. It makes sense in many ways. One's own trained personnel are returned to duty, and there is a big saving in the costs of feeding, housing, providing medical care, and policing prisoners. Conditions in prison camps on both the Union and Confederate sides were horrific. Polluted water, poor quality food, limited availability of medical care, combined with overcrowding led to high death rates from communicable diseases. Typhoid killed prisoners by the hundreds. The very unglamorous scourge of dysentery led to many deaths by extreme dehydration. There was a lot of pressure to empty the prison camps through exchanges, but President Lincoln refused to consider any such large-scale exchanges. It was well known that conditions on both sides' camps were terrible. But, Lincoln reasoned, the North had a definite advantage in the Civil War in population size, greatly outnumbering the South. A one-for-one exchange of war prisoners thus would benefit the South proportionately more than it would the North.

So the prisoners remained in the camps and died by the thousands. Is it any wonder that the Confederate ghosts of Camp Chase Cemetery are bitter and vengeful? Through the years, many people have heard faint, plaintive bugle calls at dawn and dusk in the cemetery, and some have witnessed the ghostly ranks of the boys in gray marching silently among the rows of tombstones. Should you happen to observe the phantom parade, it would be best to take off your hat when the stars and bars battle flag of the Confederacy passes by. Refusal to honor their flag can cause gray ghosts with glowing red eyes to give you a stern stare of death.

The Dead Shot

Annie Oakley was a dead shot; she also is long dead. But her spirit lives on, or so say some folks in the neighborhood of North Star, where she was born, and nearby Greenville, where she died.

Annie's ghost is friendly enough, but it is a little unnerving to meet a ghost armed with a rifle or Colt revolver. Her spirit has been known to appear when folks get to arguing as to just how good a shot she was. People say that a playing card tossed into the air will fall back with a hole or two drilled through by bullets. The misty image of a cowgirl wearing a satisfied smile listens to the faint echo of gunfire, appearing briefly before fading away.

Phoebe Ann Oakley Mozee was born in 1860 in the tiny settlement of North Star, near the Indiana line. Even as a young girl, Annie earned a reputation as a sharpshooter. She became an expert hunter and made enough money killing game to enable her to pay off the mortgage on her mother's farm by the time she was fourteen. At age fifteen, she won a shooting contest with a vaudeville marksman, Frank Butler. Frank married her a few years later and became her manager when she decided to turn professional. She was performing in a circus when she caught the eye of the renowned showman Buffalo Bill Cody. Soon she was a star in Buffalo Bill's Traveling Wild West Show.

Annie showed positively uncanny skill with guns. She could hit dimes and playing cards tossed into the air. At thirty paces, she could shoot a playing card with the thin edge toward her. When she toured Europe with Buffalo Bill, she often was asked to give private exhibitions for royalty. Once German kaiser Wilhelm II insisted that she shoot a cigarette from his lips. She did, though she didn't like to risk anyone's life as part of her tricks. Later, when America entered World War I against Germany, Annie said that for once she wished her aim had been off by a few inches.

After she was severely injured in a train wreck, she retired from show business. During World War I, she gave free shows at Army camps to entertain the troops. She died at Greenville in 1926, but her ghost, it is said, still likes to show off her shooting skills.

The Spirit of the Peaceful Warrior

This ghost is a peaceable one, never intending to frighten, but intent on warning the living. The spirit of Chief Leatherlips appears in times of strife and tension, when war clouds gather. His ghost appears to be entreating people to stop and think before charging off to war.

The peace-loving phantom usually materializes near the monument to Chief Leatherlips, which is not far from the Columbus Zoo. The monument, erected in 1888, commemorates the death of Leatherlips, executed by his fellow braves because he cautioned against an unprovoked attack on European settlers. The story is that Leatherlips argued insistently against an attack on white farmers in the vicinity, believing that it was a war the Indians were bound to lose. The westward-advancing wave of pioneers already had greatly outnumbered the Native Americans. A war, thought Leatherlips, would ultimately prove suicidal for his people. "Talk, not tomahawks," was his plea. But his was the lone voice advocating negotiations with the invaders. He would not back down from his opposition to violence. A council was held to determine his fate. Neighboring white settlers tried to intercede on Leatherlips's behalf, but that only strengthened the Indians' belief that he was a traitor to his own people or, even worse, a coward.

Leatherlips was condemned to death. Many of his white friends could not understand how a chief could be not only disobeyed, but also sentenced to die. There was a general misunderstanding of Indian leadership roles on the part of white Americans, who tended to compare Indian chiefs to European kings. Indian chiefs, however, were men, or women, who were respected for their bravery and wisdom but were expected to build a consensus, not dictate.

When, in 1810, the Wyandot Nation's Council of Chiefs decided to execute Leatherlips, he had no alternative but to accept his fate. Arrayed in full warpath splendor, he allowed himself to be led to his waiting grave, where he was dispatched by blows of tomahawks. But his spirit does not rest when violence threatens. Whenever war looms, it is said that the spirit of Leatherlips rises up, hands raised in appeal to reason, caution, and talk, not tomahawks.

The Bairdstown Curse

Most folks today in Bairdstown either don't know about the old curse on their little community or say they don't in an attempt to avoid awaking the vengeful spirit of Jim Slater. A century and a half ago, Slater put a curse on Bairdstown. Sure enough, people in the town swore that the place truly was cursed. If something could go wrong, it would.

At one time, Jim Slater owned a quarter section, or a quarter of a square mile, at the site of the town. Although Jim appeared to be a hard worker and an honest man, nothing seemed to go right for him. His corn crops failed. His cows stopped giving milk. His pigs died of mysterious diseases. His wife died in childbirth. His house burned down. He got involved in lawsuits that he inevitably lost. He lost his farm to foreclosure. Although Jim strongly protested his innocence, a neighbor's accusation that Slater had set fire to his wheatfield led to a prison sentence.

From his prison cell, Jim Slater loudly proclaimed a curse on the community of Bairdstown. Soon afterward, he was found hanging in his cell. Pinned to his chest was a note addressed to all the townspeople saying, "You'll be sorry!" It is a matter of historical fact that these events followed: The man who bought Slater's farm at a sheriff's sale built a mill that soon burned down. He eventually filed for bankruptcy. He then moved out of state, where his wife and daughter died. The next owner of the former Slater farm went insane and murdered his whole family. The lawyer who unsuccessfully defended Slater saw his entire family die in an epidemic. The prosecuting attorney died in an insane asylum. Most of the town was destroyed in a disastrous fire in 1890.

It has become a local superstition that one must never admit to knowing about Jim Slater and his curse. Recently a historian passing through town inquired about the Slater curse. Although no one even acknowledged previously hearing the name Jim Slater, the historian returned to his new car to find the battery dead and all four tires flat. Maybe you shouldn't ask about Jim Slater's curse in Bairdstown. His ghost might be listening.

Shades of the Miami Massacre

These ghosts appear only around the anniversary of the horrific incident that produced them—June 21, the approximate time of the summer solstice. The summer solstice has special mystical meaning to American Indians, as indeed it has to many peoples around the world. The summer solstice of the year 1752, though, had an atypically sinister significance for the great Miami Nation, which at one time controlled much of Western Ohio, Indiana, and Illinois.

It is just as well that the spirits of the victims of the summer solstice massacre materialize only on the anniversary of their death, as they are a particularly frightening sight. The grim events of June 21, 1752, were the results of the interconnected rivalries of Indian nations and the conflicting ambitions of the French and British empires in North America.

The Miami Nation migrated from Canada and built a fortified village called Pickawillany, near the present site of Piqua. They began trading with the English, which angered the French, who had developed a special relationship with the Miami, or so they thought. The Miami insisted on their right to trade with anyone they pleased, and their chief took the name Old Britain in tribute to their new trading partners.

When the French heard that the Miami were sheltering French deserters and hosting half a dozen English traders at Pickawillany, they sent some Indian allies under French officers to demolish the post. It was the bad luck of the Miami that fateful day that the defenders were totally unprepared. The stockade's gates were wide open, unguarded. Most Miami warriors were absent on a hunting expedition. After a brief struggle, the invaders triumphed. Then the horror began. The attackers came upon a wounded English trader. They stabbed him to death, cut off his scalp, then cut out his heart and ate it in front of their cowering foes. They seized Old Britain, the Miami chief, boiled him alive in a huge cooking pot, and ate him. Finally, they torched Pickawillany and marched the remaining Miami off to slavery in Canada.

As you can imagine, the ghosts of this atrocity are truly gruesome. The most hideous apparitions include the English trader, his scalp torn away so that his white skull gleams through the blood, with a gaping, ragged hole in his chest where his heart once beat.

Old Britain's spirit staggers on, cooked flesh falling off his steaming bones as he wails in terrible agony. The sight of these ghosts will burn itself into your memory, should you be so unlucky as to see them. Beware the summer solstice in the neighborhood of Piqua.

The Shadow of the Hawk

Most visitors to the Sherman House on East Main Street in Lancaster never see the image of the hawk. The hawk, or its shadowy ghost, appears just after dawn, hours before the historic house opens for public tours. The appearances of the hawk are so brief that if two people are standing side by side near the house, one may catch a fleeting glimpse of the great bird, while the other will swear to have seen a phantom. A local hunter once tried to shoot the great hawk that seemed to frequent his neighborhood. Armed with his shotgun, he stationed himself near the Sherman House each dawn until the bird alighted in a tree. He fired. The shotgun blast destroyed tree branches directly behind the hawk, but not a feather of the apparent ghost hawk was ruffled.

But why would the ghostly bird frequent the Sherman House? Historians and ghost hunters agree that the phantom hawk represents the soul of one of Ohio's most famous sons—William Tecumseh Sherman. The term "war hawk" has been in use for a long time to mean one who advocates war. Hawks, like their close cousins the eagles, are aggressive, courageous birds of prey. Their fierce eyes, sharp beaks, and talons reflect their alert, combative personas. A wartime photo of General Sherman, often featured in history books, shows his fierce, hawklike glare. To Northerners in the Civil War, General Sherman was a great hero, second only to General Ulysses S. Grant in his role in the defeat of the Confederacy. To Southerners, William Sherman was the devil incarnate, a ruthless terrorist who burned and pillaged his way through Georgia and the Carolinas.

William Tecumseh Sherman was born in the peaceful county seat of Lancaster, and it was to Lancaster that he returned to rest when, in the course of the war, he desperately needed a brief respite from the pressures of leading an army. Lancaster always represented a safe haven to Sherman, which might explain why his spirit, symbolized by a great hawk, still abides there.

The hawk is a proud bird, again making it a perfect symbol of the general. Sherman, a great admirer of Lincoln, was well aware that his timely capture of Atlanta was instrumental in assuring the president's reelection in 1864. In late December of that year, Sherman gleefully telegraphed Lincoln that he had a Christmas present for him—the city of Savannah, newly captured. Apparently Sherman's spirit still flies high, if you are lucky enough to see the phantom hawk of Lancaster.

Second Sight

Many years ago, a resident of Lancaster was blessed with second sight, the ability to see into the future. Or was it really a case of being cursed by second sight? There is an ancient tradition that persons born with a caul—that is, born still enveloped in the placental lining membrane—will have the gift of second sight. Mary Jane Anderson was such a person, though in time she came to regard second sight as a very problematic "gift."

As a young child, Mary Jane began showing signs of second sight. Once, at a Christmas dinner attended by all her relatives, she gave her grandfather a big hug as he prepared to go home. "Goodbye, Grandpa," she said. "You will soon see Grandma again. Give her our love, and don't be afraid." Grandma had died four years previously. Mary Jane's farewell to her grandfather was dismissed as the confused thinking of a child. Until, that is, Grandpa died suddenly of a stroke three days later. The little girl was questioned as to how she knew of Grandpa's impeding death. "I saw it happen" was her calm reply.

Mary Jane began to be treated with a certain amount of awe, tinged with a little fear. What would she "see" next? The Anderson household began to be harassed by people seeking to take advantage of Mary Jane's second sight. Would railroad stock be a good investment? What would be the price of hogs next year? Would the local bank fail? The poor girl was overwhelmed with questions about the future. Some shameless townspeople even wanted predictions of deaths so that they could buy insurance policies on healthy young people who would soon die.

The girl resisted most pressures to use her supernatural sight for financial gain. She believed that her gift of second sight came from

God and should not be abused out of greed. But then the Anderson family farm ran into money problems. The price of corn fell because, ironically, favorable weather produced record yields and drove down prices. The family could not pay a large mortgage payment due to the bank in time to avoid a foreclosure, or so it seemed. Mary Jane gave in to temptation. In one of her visions of the future, she saw a newspaper headline: "Price of hogs rises sharply." The Andersons borrowed money and bought young pigs, as many as they could. Sure enough, within a few months, rising demand multiplied their value, and the farm was saved.

There was one problem, however. The Devil showed up one midnight. "You have placed yourself in my power," he gloated. "You've misused your God-given powers of second sight for personal gain, and now your soul belongs to me." "But this was not just for personal gain," replied Mary Jane. "I advised all our neighbors to invest in pigs as well, and we all pledged to tithe to our churches." Mary Jane then pointed out that she was surrounded by twelve Holy Bibles. As the Devil shrank back, she tossed a pan of holy water on him, causing him to writhe in pain. "You forgot," she yelled after the hastily retreating Satan, "that I have second sight. I foresaw your coming and prepared for it."

It is said that Mary Jane never again told anyone of her visions of the future, nor did she ever again take action on the basis of her second sight. And the Devil never bothered her again, either.

Eastern Heartland

THIS LARGE REGION, WELL POPULATED BY PHANTOMS, CONSISTS OF THE area east of Columbus. One of the many interesting aspects of ghost stories is that not all spirits are negative or threatening. From the Eastern Heartland, for example, come tales of the spirit of a clergyman whose long-winded prayer probably saved a life, a patriotic ghost, and the Devil himself being outsmarted for once. For fans of scary ghost stories, the region also features a gruesomely haunted old inn, spirits from a long-ago massacre, and the phantoms of a tragic mine accident.

Ghostly Moans of the Millfield Miners

Sometimes the restless spirits of those who died in agonizing terror manifest in the world of the living as sounds rather than as visible apparitions. So it is with the eighty-two victims of a long-ago but not forgotten mine disaster at the tiny town of Millfield.

Ever since the terrible events of November 5, 1930, many have reported hearing the sound of tortured, strangled gasping for breath, punctuated by hoarse screams for help. Surely slow suffocation, trapped far underground, is one of the most excruciating deaths anyone could suffer. As the available oxygen is used up, the victim

becomes ever more aware of the desperation of the situation and the inevitability of his or her fate. The chest muscles expand the lungs in a frantic though hopeless attempt to gain sufficient oxygen. Eventually the oxygen-starved brain begins to shut down, and the helpless victim loses consciousness. Imagine hearing your workmates and friends around you gasping their last breaths, knowing that you will soon follow them in death.

It was midday when an explosion ripped through Mine No. 6 of the Sunday Creek Coal Company. There was an unusually large group of men in the mine that day as, ironically, the company president had led a team of eight executives into the mine on an inspection tour. There had been reports from concerned miners that safety rules were ignored routinely. Underground coal mining is one of the most dangerous occupations imaginable. Inadequate ventilation can allow dangerous buildups of coal dust, which can explode when provided with a tiny spark. Fires, once started, can burn for decades, sucking up all available oxygen. Tunnel collapses can trap miners deep beneath the surface, sentencing them to painfully slow deaths by suffocation.

It was evening, eight hours after the noon explosion, when rescue crews finally broke through the debris-clogged collapsed tunnels to reach the trapped miners. They were all dead. It was reported that the would-be rescuers recoiled in horror when they saw the agonized grimaces on the victims' faces. They had soul-wrenching nightmares about those tortured faces for the rest of their lives.

To this day, as dusk approaches earlier and earlier in late fall, some hear the faint sounds of protracted, painful gasping for breath amid the quiet of the little river valley, as the pitiful spirits of the dead miners apparently relive their last hopeless, agonizing moments of life. Say a brief prayer for their tormented souls, or at least a wish that their tormented souls might find peace at last.

Toasting a Hanging

Some old-timers in Newark claim that the town square once hosted an odd pair of spirits, with frequent materializations in the summer months. These two ghosts always appeared together, though they haven't been seen in recent years. One phantom hanged from a large tree limb, while the other stood close by, a large beer stein raised high as though toasting the hanged man. Although they met only briefly in life, the two spirits seemed to be united in the spirit world, or so it appeared for decades after their violent deaths. The ghost holding aloft his stein had been murdered, the victim of the man who, hours later, was brought to rough justice by a vengeful mob.

In the early 1900s, there had been a long, bitter struggle between Americans who were determined to outlaw alcoholic beverages and those citizens who liked a drink now and then. Ohio passed a local option law, allowing each county's voters to decide whether the county would be wet or dry. Licking County narrowly voted dry, although Newark, the county seat, was enthusiastically wet. The local glassworks, which had manufactured beer bottles, closed its doors as the drys triumphed. As a result, a lot of Newarkers were out of work. Townspeople chose to ignore the fact that their county had gone dry, and saloons continued in operation, openly tolerated by local law enforcement.

On July 10, 1910, the powerful antisaloon league hired twenty-three private detectives, had them deputized by a friendly judge, and sent them into Newark to enforce the law and shut the saloons. These "dry detectives" definitely were not welcome in Newark. When a rumor spread that a popular local bartender had been slugged, a mob gathered, threatening vengeance. A dry detective was trapped in a downtown bar. In a panic, he shot and killed the saloon keeper. His fellow detectives fled for their lives. A mob fueled by a few drinks descended on the jail where the murderer was being held. The sheriff telephoned the governor, asking him to call out the National Guard to protect his prisoner, but it was too late. A mob estimated at five thousand stormed the jail, kidnapped the culprit, and hanged him from a handy tree. The bloody body of the slain saloon keeper was brought to the town square and propped up against the tree trunk beneath the swinging corpse of his murderer. Many a man raised a glass in toast to justice and the right of adults to enjoy a drink.

In the increasingly unlikely event that you should witness the appearance of these two ghosts, it would be advisable to raise your glass in a toast.

Strike! Strike!

The Market Street Bridge across the Mahoning River in downtown Youngstown has been the scene of a very unusual ghostly parade, though few have witnessed the manifestation in recent years. Perhaps the ghosts involved in this gruesome parade finally are finding peace, for the event that apparently created them is now more than seventy years in the past.

When last reportedly seen by the living, the supernatural demonstration consisted of scores of men choking and gasping for breath as they marched over the bridge near midnight, usually on a foggy, rainy night. Some of the phantom marchers were bleeding from what appeared to be bullet holes, and they carried on their shoulders two coffins. Oddly, the coffins were lidless, and in each a bloody corpse was seen sitting up, holding a large, homemade sign saying, "Strike!" "Strike! Strike!" chanted the misty images of the angry workers. And then, just as it seemed that the parade of shadows was about to collide with a living person or a vehicle, the ghosts all faded away and there was nothing left of the phantom parade.

Old-timers and local historians agree that these now seldom seen phantoms were the ghosts of an important and tragic event in the history of American labor unions and industrial strife. Ohio has witnessed some bitter industrial strikes in its long history as a leading manufacturing state. The Great Depression of the 1930s hit Ohio's northern manufacturing belt—Cleveland, Youngstown, Akron, and Toledo—especially hard. Scores of thousands of workers lost their jobs. Unable to pay mortgages and taxes, many families were forced out of their homes. Bankrupt farmers lost their farms. Small businesses closed.

Following prolonged strikes, the major steel manufacturers, "big steel," agreed to recognize unions and negotiate labor contracts. But the smaller, independent companies, "little steel," held out. Fifty thousand workers went on strike. When Republic Steel at Youngstown tried to break the strike, a riot broke out. Two strikers were killed and twenty-seven were wounded by gunfire. Hundreds were sickened by clouds of tear gas. The National Guard was called out to supervise a tense truce until the strike could be settled.

Youngstown's "little steel" strike was a low point in national labor relations. The dead and wounded strikers became martyrs to their cause. And according to some, they became ghosts as well.

The Chief Who Lost His Head

Near the town of West Salem lies a beautiful little valley named after Chief Kattotowa, who is buried nearby. At least most of Chief Kattotowa is buried on Boots Farm, for legend says that his head is missing. To this day, people in the area avoid the Kattotowa Valley on foggy nights lest they meet the headless ghost of the chief.

There are several versions of the story of how Chief Kattotowa lost his head. The most romantic variation has him losing his head over a beautiful woman and a quest for peace.

Kattotowa was said to have been a chief of the Delaware tribe, which had migrated into this part of Ohio, fleeing both the advancing whites and the hostile tribes of the Iroquois Confederacy. These tribes had first invaded Ohio from Canada and the Northeast starting in the mid-seventeenth century.

Chief Kattotowa argued that it would be suicidal for the Delaware to try to fight both the invading whites and the Iroquoian people. He envisioned a grand alliance of tribes to present a united front in negotiating with, or if necessary fighting, invading white settlers. The ancient and bitter enmity among tribes must be buried, as he saw it.

There was a long-standing tradition of not intermarrying between tribes. A beautiful woman from the Tuscarora people had caught Kattotowa's eye, a certain Princess Sunflower. What better way to symbolize burying the rivalries of the past and cementing a new alliance than an intertribal marriage? Sunflower readily agreed to become the wife of the handsome Kattotowa. But Sunflower's parents, and indeed her whole tribe, were strongly opposed.

Bravely but foolishly, Kattotowa went to Sunflower's people to plead his case. "You must cast your eyes away from Sunflower," warned her father. "You are risking death." Chief Kattotowa stubbornly declared his undying love for Sunflower, whose brothers then seized him and decapitated him with a tomahawk.

Kattotowa's head was thrust into a campfire, but even as it burned, his headless body strode out of camp, or so the story goes.

The chief's determination to marry his beloved couldn't be deterred by a mere beheading. His headless ghost still walks the valley looking for Sunflower, and for peace among his peoples.

The Mystery of the Tombstone Snakes

The cemetery of the tiny community of North Benton contains a unique grave marker. Atop the grave of one Chester Bedell, who departed this life in 1908, is a lifesize bronze male figure. Under his foot is crushed a scroll titled, "Superstition," while his upraised hand brandishes a scroll inscribed, "Universal Mental Liberty." The bronze statue itself would draw attention, but what makes this grave really interesting is the curse said to have been placed on it.

Chester Bedell, it seems, was a rather colorful character in his tiny community. Some locals called him a free thinker, others an agnostic. A few called him very unflattering names that do not bear repeating. Chester doubted the existence of God, and he said so loudly and often. "Where is the proof?" demanded Bedell. "How do we know that God exists?" His neighbors no doubt prayed for him and erected more lightning rods on property adjacent to that belonging to Bedell.

When he clearly was close to death, Chester issued a public challenge to the ruler of the universe: "If God is real, let him place snakes on my grave." Locals claim that the grave diggers uncovered a huge nest of rattlesnakes when opening Bedell's final resting spot. They spent a frantic hour beheading snakes with their spades.

Snakes have continued to hang out, so to speak, atop Chester Bedell's grave. The creepy crawlers have been seen writhing about the base of his rather defiant grave marker. Many a mourner at other graves nearby has heard the distinctive buzz of the rattlesnake's trademark warning coming from Bedell's plot.

Many locals believe that the snakes, both dead and alive, frequently seen draped over the bronze figure were placed there by neighborhood boys to perpetuate Chester's notoriety. However they got there, the serpents seem to be a permanent feature of the doubter's grave. Should you decide to see for yourself, approach Chester Bedell's cursed grave carefully, listening for rattles.

The Cursed Wayfarers' Inn

The old National Road once played a major role in settling the Midwest. It jump-started the growth of many towns along the way as it extended across Ohio in the years between 1825 and 1838. Scores of thousands of travelers crossed Ohio by stagecoach. A few never completed their journey, victims of road accidents, highway bandits, or in the case of Middlebourne's infamous Locust Lodge, ruthless innkeepers. Way back when it was known as Hayes Tavern, this wayfarers' inn was a death trap for unwary and wealthy travelers.

Congress authorized the construction of a paved road westward from Cumberland, Maryland, to Wheeling, West Virginia, in 1806. The goal was to provide a highway across the Appalachians to facilitate western migration and trade. In 1825, an extension west from Wheeling to Illinois was approved. The road reached Zanesville in 1826, Columbus by 1833, and Springfield in 1838.

Eyewitness accounts tell of as many as twenty-five stagecoaches in a row carrying passengers westward, along with scores of heavy freight wagons. Inns sprang up to provide bed, food, drink, and a little entertainment for travelers, along with the care and feeding of horses and oxen. Some innkeepers became wealthy as traffic surged in the westward expansion.

Hayes Tavern was built in Middlebourne sometime in the late 1820s. For a while, it was a highly respected inn, operated for a time by a descendant of Pennsylvania's Penn family. Such national figures as Henry Clay chose it for a night's rest. As riverboats and then railroads competed successfully for travelers, however, business began to dwindle at the roadside inns. Some went out of business. At Hayes Tavern, later renamed the Locust Lodge, a ruthless innkeeper began to increase profits through robbery and murder.

In those days, there was no such thing as credit cards, and checks were not accepted where banks were few and far away. Travelers on the National Road needed to carry gold and silver coins, enough to pay for weeks on the road.

Solitary guests at the Locust Lodge who unwisely flashed wallets bulging with gold often were led to a room without windows. As soon as they entered, they were knocked unconscious, then their throats were cut with a sharp razor. The corpses were disposed of in the nearby woods, where packs of wild dogs were said to have quickly disposed of their flesh. The windowless murder room, its floor and walls soaked repeatedly in innocent blood, became known as the "dark room." The legend grew that Locust Lodge was cursed, and that bloody corpses haunted its rooms. The "dark room" was said to actually ooze blood from its flooring and wall paneling. Screams, it is claimed, echoed from that room of horror.

The innkeeper never was brought to trial, but public opinion condemned Locust Lodge. Abandoned, it slowly decayed by the side of the road, a symbol of satanic "hospitality."

The Murderous Newcomer

The little community of Newcomerstown near Cosholton is the site of occasional appearances of a rather scary ghost, the spirit of the "newcomer" for whom the village was named, the second wife of Chief Eagle Feather and also his murderer. Some have reported seeing the ghost of a beautiful young Indian woman, with an angry determined expression and brandishing a bloodstained tomahawk.

Newcomerstown once was an important Indian settlement called Gekelemukpechunk; it served as the capital of the Delaware tribe. The story is that Mary Harris, a white woman from New England, was brought here as a captive by Indian warriors. She is supposed to have been the first white woman seen in this part of Ohio. Mary's blond beauty attracted the attention of Chief Eagle Feather, who made her his wife. Apparently it was a good marriage, and Mary cheerfully settled down and raised several children, adapting well to Indian lifestyles and customs.

One local custom, however, displeased Mary, and that was the habit of powerful chiefs to take more than one wife. About ten years after Mary married Eagle Feather, another comely captive was brought into camp. She was a lovely young maiden captured from a neighboring tribe. Her real name is lost in the mists of history, as everyone called her the newcomer, a name assigned by Mary Harris when her husband decided to add a second wife to his household.

Mary very much resented this newcomer. Mary had been a good wife and a good mother. She had learned her tribe's language and culture, even its cooking style. As the first wife, she was in charge of her husband's household. She assigned the newcomer the dirtiest, hardest chores, making her as miserable as possible. Worse,

Mary spread false stories about the newcomer, accusing her of infidelity and witchcraft. As Mary had planned, Eagle Feather heard the malicious gossip and began wondering whether his second wife really could be a witch. When the chief's favorite hunting dog went mad and had to be destroyed, Mary blamed the newcomer's curse. When a neighbor who disliked the newcomer lost her house to a lightning strike, it must have been the newcomer's revenge. Was the sudden death of the household's cow a malicious gesture of the newcomer? Skillfully, Mary wove a blanket of suspicion and mistrust about the newcomer.

Blamed for any ill luck or accident, isolated in an increasingly hostile community, scorned by her husband's clever first wife, and increasingly ignored by her bridegroom, the newcomer grew paranoid. When Eagle Feather was discovered hacked to bloody pieces one morning, suspicion fell immediately on the newcomer, who had fled into the woods. Cornered by a search party, the newcomer still carried a bloody tomahawk.

The unrepentant newcomer was hanged that same day. Her ghost, it is said, still walks the lonely country roads, carrying the death weapon high above her head. Beware this ghost, still violent in her rage against Chief Eagle Feather and his clever, manipulative white wife. There are those who wonder whether Mary Harris was the real witch in this story.

The Devil and the S Bridges

The oldest section of the National Road as it traverses Ohio lies between Bridgeport and Zanesville. A curiosity of this old road, long since paralleled and replaced by U.S. Route 40 and more recently Interstate 70, was the construction of stone bridges in the shape of a large letter S.

No one is sure why this unusual design was chosen. Stone arch bridges are not the easiest construction projects, so why make them more difficult and expensive to construct? The shallow reversing curves slow down traffic, but excessive speed could not have been a problem in the days of Conestoga wagons. The S curve of the roadway does not produce either a stronger or safer bridge. Some attempts at explaining the S bridges are just plain silly. One suggestion was that the builders didn't want to bother cutting down large trees growing along stream banks, so they routed the bridges around them. Another, not entirely unlikely given the drinking habits of some engineers, was that the design was a product of a bar bet during a night of hard drinking.

Chances are, however, that there simply is no explanation in logic or rational thinking by engineers. The answer probably lies in so-called white magic as opposed to black or evil magic or witchcraft. The Devil, it is alleged, likes to travel in straight lines. The Lord of the Underworld also is reluctant to cross water, unless on a sturdy bridge so that he won't get his feet wet. Old Satan moves quickly, as in the phrase "run like the devil." When the Devil is chasing down a sinful soul, intent on dragging it down into hell, he travels as fast as his legs can carry him. The real purpose of the S bridges was to frustrate Satan, as the Prince of Darkness, running full tilt after a sinner, would fail to negotiate the unexpected curve and thus slam into the side of the stone walls, knocking him senseless at least briefly.

At the few surviving S bridges, no longer used for highway traffic, such as Middlebourne, it is said that one can still see the scuff marks where the Devil missed the curve and hit the wall. So now you know.

The Ghost of the Frustrated Diplomat

Near the little town of Lucas is a picturesque rock formation overlooking the valley of the Mohican River. It is known as Pipe's Cliff, and it is, on occasion, haunted.

A misty apparition has been known to appear on Pipe's Cliff at dawn. The spirit is that of an Indian chief, facing the rising sun, following an ancient Indian custom of greeting the new day with a prayer. In this instance, it's believed that in addition to the prayer for the new day, this phantom was also praying for the spirit of a dead sister, murdered here by a white scouting party back in the 1780s.

The ghostly figure kneeling in prayer is thought to be the shade of Chief Hopocan, who also was known to whites as "Captain Pipe." His slain sister, Onalaska, is said to be memorialized by a solitary rock, thirty feet in height, that rises from the cliff's edge.

Chief Hopocan was a frustrated diplomat. He came by his nickname, Captain Pipe, because for years he met westward-moving whites with a peace pipe, ready to negotiate disputes about land and Indian rights. Repeatedly, he tried to talk out problems rather than resort to violence. Repeatedly, whites broke treaties and agreements, even refusing to talk at all on occasion.

Hopocan began to wonder whether his peace pipe shouldn't be replaced by a tomahawk. The event that finally persuaded him to take the path of war rather than talk was the unprovoked murder of his beloved sister, Onalaska. A group of whites came upon a group of Indians, including Onalaska, resting atop the promontory since named Pipe's Cliff. Without warning or cause, the whites shot all of the Indians.

When Hopocan heard about this, he decided to lead attacks on the whites invading Indian lands. He later boasted that he "tomahawked whites until his arm ached." He put down his tomahawk only when the Greenville Treaty of Peace between Indians and whites was signed in 1795, living in peace until his death in 1812.

Those who have seen his ghost atop Pipe's Cliff report that the spirit holds a peace pipe in one hand and a tomahawk in the other. In death as in life, Captain Pipe is ready to talk or go to war, as the occasion demands.

The Lexington Serpent

Are you afraid of snakes? Join the club. Many people have a deep, unreasoning fear of snakes, perhaps a genetic survivor of primitive humankind's very real terror of serpents. It is not a coincidence that the book of Genesis introduced Satan in the form of a snake. Perhaps it is the blank, emotionless eyes of snakes that frighten us, along with the ability of poisonous reptiles to deal agonizing death.

Beginning in the nineteenth century, sightings of an enormous, aggressive serpent in a swampy area near Lexington have been reported. Although most encounters with the huge serpent took place more than a century ago, a few claim to have spotted this monster more recently. Is it the same snake or the ghost of one? No one who has seen the giant snake wanted to get close enough or stay around long enough to determine whether it was alive or a ghost. This is understandable, as the snake, or its ghost, is reported to be at least twenty feet long. Was it, or is it, even longer? Nineteenth-century cynics said that the infamous Lexington serpent was so stretchable in description that it must be made of rubber. Supposedly, when the subject of the serpent came up in a local tavern, the length of the snake grew in proportion to the number of drinks consumed by the one telling the story. The ratio was alleged to be an increase of three feet in length for every drink downed.

Other than its somewhat flexible length, the Lexington serpent has been described as having large red eyes; a purple forked tongue; a speckled black, yellow, and green body; and curiously, several tails. It is said to have a huge appetite, pursuing, catching, and swallowing whole pigs, cows, and sheep. Some claim that it had, or has, a row of sharp spines along its back.

Does this vicious serpent, or its ghost, still stalk its prey around Lexington? Did it ever exist outside the imagination of people who'd had a few too many drinks? Should you hear tales of the great snake in a bar some evening, buy the storyteller a drink and see if the serpent's description expands with alcohol.

The Trembling First Lady

This pathetic ghost is seldom seen these days, though it once was a fairly commonly reported apparition. Perhaps her spirit finally has found peace a century after her death, for this is the ghost of Ida Saxton McKinley, widow of the twenty-fifth president of the United States, William McKinley. Hers is a nonthreatening, gentle ghost that evokes only sympathy in the hearts of any who see it, especially those familiar with her story.

Ida Saxton was the sophisticated, well-educated daughter of a banker when she met William McKinley, a young ambitious lawyer and Civil War hero. The young couple's married life was clouded by tragedy, as both their daughters died early in their lives. It is said that the trauma of losing her second offspring at the age of five months brought about the first of a lifetime of epileptic seizures and fragile health for Ida. The stresses of the White House social life were particularly hard on her. She customarily clutched a small bouquet while seated in a chair in a receiving line so that she wouldn't have to shake hands, revealing her trembling limbs. When, as happened often at state dinners, she passed out briefly, eyes rolling back in her head, her husband would place a handkerchief over her stricken face and continue conversation. Guests would politely ignore the incident until her recovery. The president always was tenderly protective of her. When he was gunned down in Buffalo in 1902, McKinley's first words to an aide as he lay in a pool of blood were about his concern for his wife. "Be careful how you tell her," he whispered to his secretary. "She's not strong, you know."

Ida outlived her assassinated husband by six years and eventually was buried beside him and their infant daughters. Her ghost is said to sit by the graves of her husband and children, holding a bouquet and trembling visibly. Should you see her grieving spirit, avert your eyes from her handicap.

The Most Patriotic Ghost

The tiny community of Hiramsburg contains the grave of the man believed to be the longest-living person to have served in George Washington's Revolutionary armies. His tombstone reads: "John Gray, died March 29, 1868, aged 104 years, 2 months, 23 days. The last of Washington's companions. The hoary head is a crown of glory."

But what makes John Gray's grave unusual is not just his advanced age or his association with the father of our country. John Gray's spirit is said to materialize by his tombstone on patriotic holidays—Memorial Day, the Fourth of July, Veterans Day, and of course, Washington's Birthday. On these special occasions, Gray's ghost, dressed in his Revolutionary War uniform, has been seen just after dawn as the American flag is raised to the top of the flagpole. The shimmering, misty figure comes to attention, salutes the flag, then just evaporates.

John Gray's story truly is remarkable. He was born near Mount Vernon in 1764 and worked on George Washington's estate as a youth. As a teenager, he joined Washington's army and saw service in Virginia in the last days of the war. Gray always claimed that he played an important, if minor, role in the British surrender at Yorktown, though there is no written documentation of this. It is known that General Washington broke with military tradition when he accepted British general Lord Cornwallis's surrender. Protocol suggested that the surrender document be delivered in person by General Cornwallis to his equal-rank counterpart in the American Army, which would have been General Washington. This custom later was followed at Appomattox Courthouse, where General Grant personally received General Lee, for example.

But George Washington was tired of the hypocritical, phony gestures of the aristocratic British generals who had scorned and mocked him throughout the war. Washington observed that while they pretended to be honorable gentlemen, the British commanders didn't hesitate to steal, at gunpoint, livestock and grain from innocent farmers along their line of march. Some gentlemen! Some sense of honor!

General Washington decided to send in his stead an ordinary, humble, loyal American soldier to receive the surrender document. So as military bands played the appropriate tune, "The World Turned Upside Down," Corporal John Gray went to see General Cornwallis. "Cornwallis wouldn't shake my hand!" gleefully reported Corporal Gray to General Washington. "Good!" replied Washington. "He is not worthy of a good American soldier."

It is said that if cemetery visitors whistle or hum the national anthem, even on nonholidays, the shade of Corporal Gray will appear briefly to salute them. You might try that if you visit his grave and don't mind seeing a ghost.

Does John Brown's Body Still Moulder in His Grave?

John Brown's body, as the song popular during the Civil War repeated, lies mouldering in his grave. But his spirit lives on, apparently in more than one sense. A house once rented by the notorious abolitionist in Akron is open to public tours. Some visitors claim to sense a presence, a barely visible manifestation of the spirit of John Brown. Brown was a highly controversial activist in his life, and the arguments continue a century and a half after his death by hanging.

Many of those who claim they've seen John Brown's ghost at his onetime home on Diagonal Road in Akron say that only his head becomes visible as a faintly glowing, misty apparition. John Brown's fiercely staring eyes, almost hypnotic in their intensity, are the truly scary feature of his ghost, as they were of the living man.

John Brown was born in Torrington, Connecticut, in 1800 but spent part of his adult life in Ohio, living in Hudson, Richfield, near

Cleveland, and in Akron. At one time, he planned to become a minister, but he soon abandoned his studies. During his Ohio period, Brown pursued varied careers: surveying, leather tanning, sheep raising, and selling wool. He seemed to be one of those people who just couldn't settle into a job or profession. He went bankrupt at the close of his Akron sojourn and later lived in Kansas and New York State.

Brown shocked the nation when he and a small band of followers attacked the U.S. arsenal at Harpers Ferry, which was an important rifle-manufacturing center. His plan was to arm fugitive slaves and set up a free state in the mountains of western Virginia. Soldiers led by Robert E. Lee captured Brown, and he was put on trial for treason. The city of Cleveland sent its smartest lawyer to defend John Brown, and the city of Akron also contributed to his defense. When Brown was hanged, many Ohio towns lowered their flags to half-mast and tolled church bells. In death, the noble freedom fighter or ruthless, insane terrorist—take your pick—became a symbol of the crisis that became the Civil War.

His glowering face full of righteous anger still strikes both fear and admiration in the hearts of those who have glimpsed it briefly in his Akron house. Beware his tormented ghost, for John Brown apparently is still outraged that the United States once tolerated human slavery.

The Shadow of the Shenandoah

A strange phenomenon occasionally haunts the old coal-mining country of southeastern Ohio. The area between Cambridge and Sharon is the most likely scene of an unforgettable experience—an encounter with a ghostly airship. Although some have thought that this phantom of the skies was a UFO, it is much more likely that the phenomenon is related to the tragic crash of the *Shenandoah* on September 2, 1925.

Everyone has heard of the spectacular end of the German airship *Hindenburg* at Lakehurst, New Jersey, on May 6, 1937. That disaster was filmed by a newsreel crew, which recorded this fiery end of airships as luxury passenger carriers. *Hindenburg*'s end was blamed on the German use of flammable hydrogen to inflate their giant dirigible, whereas American airships were buoyed by much safer helium gas.

From World War I through the 1930s, there was a great deal of interest in dirigibles, which in contrast to blimps had rigid frameworks of aluminum girders to contain the giant gasbags or balloons that made the airships actually lighter than air. Germany and Ohio were the centers of airship research, and the hangars at Akron once were the largest buildings in the world without interior supports. At a time when airplanes could fly only relatively short distances, dirigibles could cruise across oceans. The German airship *Graf Zeppelin*, for example, completed a round-the-world voyage in 1929.

The U.S. Navy built and operated airships for military purposes, as, unlike airplanes, they not only had enormous cruising range, but also could hover like giant helicopters while searching for submarines. Even with the use of nonflammable helium, however, airships had a fatal flaw: Their great bulk and slow speed made it difficult to control them in thunderstorms.

The Navy's airship *Shenandoah* was over southeastern Ohio when it was caught in a massive storm. Violent winds tore it apart in the skies, and a large section crashed to earth at the tiny town of Ava, killing its commander and thirteen other crewmembers. A smaller section drifted down at Sharon, where farmers were able to snag a trailing cable and tie it down, saving the remaining crew.

To this day, many have reported being suddenly shadowed by a huge, cigar-shaped black image on the ground. But when they look up, there is nothing in the blue sky that could have cast the shadow. Was it the ghost of the doomed *Shenandoah* flying over them?

Bibliography

Atwater, Caleb. *A History of the State of Ohio.* Cincinnati: Glezen and Shepard, 1838.

Botkin, B. A., ed. *A Treasury of American Folklore.* New York: Crown, 1944.

Clark, Jerome. *Unexplained.* Canton, MI: Visible Ink, 1999.

Cohen, Daniel. *Railway Ghosts and Highway Horrors.* New York: Scholastic Books, 1991.

Coleman, Loren. *Mysterious America.* London: Faber and Faber, 1983.

Dorson, Richard. *American Folklore.* Chicago: University of Chicago Press, 1959.

Federal Writers' Program. *The Ohio Guide.* New York: Oxford University Press, 1940. Reprint, 1962.

Guiley, Rosemary. *The Encyclopedia of Ghosts and Spirits.* New York: Facts on File, 1992.

Harper, Charles. *Haunted Houses: Tales of the Supernatural.* Philadelphia: J. B. Lippincott, 1930.

Hatcher, Harlan. *The Buckeye Country.* New York: H. C. Kinsey, 1940.

Hauck, Dennis. *Haunted Places: The National Directory.* New York: Penguin, 2002.

Hildreth, Samuel. *Contributions to the Early History of the Northwest.* Cincinnati: Poe and Hitchcock, 1864.

Howe, Henry. *Historical Collections of Ohio.* 2 vols. Cincinnati: State of Ohio, 1904.

Hulbert, Archer. *The Ohio River: A Course of Empire.* New York: G. P. Putnam, 1906.

Krantz, Les. *America by the Numbers: Facts and Figures from the Weighty to the Way-Out.* Boston: Houghton Mifflin, 1993.

Martzolff, Clement. *Fifty Stories from Ohio History.* Columbus: Teacher Publishing, 1917.

Myers, Arthur. *The Ghostly Register*. New York: McGraw-Hill/Contemporary Books, 1986.

Pickering, David. *Cassell Dictionary of Superstitions*. London: Cassell, 1995.

Roseboom, Eugene, and Francis Weisenburger. *A History of Ohio*. New York: Prentice Hall, 1934.

Shetrone, Henry. *The Mound Builders*. New York: D. Appleton, 1930.

Skinner, Charles. *American Myths and Legends*. Detroit: Gale Research, 1974.

Taylor, Troy. *The Haunting of America: Ghosts and Legends from America's Past*. Alton, IL: White Chapel, 2001.

Acknowledgments

I THANK KYLE WEAVER, MY SKILLFUL AND SUPPORTIVE EDITOR, FOR HIS enthusiastic encouragement on this, our sixth book together. His assistant, Brett Keener, capably handled the many details during production. As in earlier volumes, the delightfully atmospheric illustrations are the creative products of Heather Adel Wiggins.

My colleague at Rowan University, Laura Ruthig, once again managed to produce a coherent manuscript out of my untidy, nearly indecipherable handwriting. Thanks again for your friendship and assistance.

My dear wife, Diane, patiently endured my ongoing preoccupation with research and writing. As ever, my heartfelt thanks go to my soulmate and constant companion on our life journeys.

About the Author

CHARLES A. STANSFIELD JR. TAUGHT GEOGRAPHY AT ROWAN UNIVER-sity for forty-one years and published fifteen textbooks on cultural and regional geography. In the course of his research, he realized that stories of ghosts and other strange phenomena reflect the history, culture, economy, and even physical geography of a region. He is the author of *Haunted Vermont, Haunted Maine,* and *Haunted Jersey Shore* and coauthor with Patricia A. Martinelli of *Haunted New Jersey.*

Other Titles in the
Haunted Series

HAUNTED CONNECTICUT
by Cheri Revai • 978-0-8117-3296-3

HAUNTED DELAWARE
by Patricia A. Martinelli • 978-0-8117-3297-0

HAUNTED ILLINOIS
by Troy Taylor • 978-0-8117-3499-8

HAUNTED MARYLAND
by Ed Okonowicz • 978-0-8117-3409-7

HAUNTED MASSACHUSETTS
by Cheri Revai • 978-0-8117-3221-5

HAUNTED NEW YORK
by Cheri Revai • 978-0-8117-3249-9

**HAUNTED
NEW YORK CITY**
by Cheri Revai • 978-0-8117-3471-4

HAUNTED PENNSYLVANIA
by Mark Nesbitt and Patty A. Wilson
978-0-8117-3298-7

HAUNTED WEST VIRGINIA
by Patty A. Wilson • 978-0-8117-3400-4

WWW.STACKPOLEBOOKS.COM • 1-800-732-3669